Problem Solving

Years 3-4

Pete Hall

Published by Hopscotch
A division of MA Education Ltd
St Jude's Church
Dulwich Road
Herne Hill
London SE24 0PB

Tel: 020 7738 5454

Written by Pete Hall
Series design by Blade Communications
Layout and graphics by Norman Brownsword
Cover illustration by Susan Hutchison
Illustrated by Bernard Connors
Printed in the UK by CLE, St Ives, Huntingdon, Cambridgeshire

ISBN 1902239199
ISBN13 978-1-902239-19-4

Problem Solving

Years 3-4

'The ability to solve problems is at the heart of mathematics.'

Mathematics Counts 1982

Problem solving has always been an important but neglected element of mathematics. Far too much of mathematics teaching concentrated on the practice and consolidation of number skills in isolation from the broader context, ie why we needed to learn the skills. The introduction of the National Curriculum for mathematics, with its emphasis on 'Using and applying' was a forward step. However, since the launch of the National Numeracy Strategy and the *Framework for Teaching Mathematics* there appears to have been a decline in the emphasis on problem solving. Indeed the HMI Evaluation of the National Numeracy Strategy (2001) reports that, 'in the main teaching activity, problem solving is still underemphasised'.

This book offers 18 problem-solving lessons. Each lesson combines teaching objectives from the Solving problems section of the *Framework for Teaching Mathematics* with objectives from the general sections. This approach will provide more time within the mathematics curriculum because objectives are combined and linked. Each lesson is aimed at providing children with a challenging learning experience with the emphasis on enjoyment. Mathematics is a wonderfully exciting and rewarding subject and it is vital as teachers that we communicate this to our children.

Problem-solving qualities

In order to make progress in problem-solving activities children need to develop a range of skills or qualities that are not specific to mathematics. Many children can find problem solving very daunting because they have not developed these necessary qualities. Therefore it is vital that schools start to develop them in Key Stage 1 and continue to develop them throughout the children's school careers. Schools should discuss how they could develop these necessary qualities, which include the following.

- The ability to discuss, work cooperatively and work individually.
- The ability to communicate using mathematics.
- The ability to define and understand problems.
- The ability to think of key questions.
- The ability to explore and experiment.
- The ability to recognise 'blind alleys'.
- The ability to develop 'transfer skills'.
- The ability to use imagination and flexibility of mind.
- The ability to be reflective.
- The ability to persevere.

Mathematical problem-solving skills

In addition to the generic qualities listed above, the National Curriculum lists these skills.

Using and applying number

Pupils should be taught to:

Problem solving

a) Approach problems involving number, and data presented in a variety of forms, in order to identify what they need to do.
b) Develop flexible approaches to problem solving and look for ways to overcome difficulties.
c) Make decisions about which operations and problem-solving strategies to use.
d) Organise and check their work.

Communicating

e) Use the correct language, symbols and vocabulary associated with number and data.
f) Communicate in spoken, pictorial and written form, at first using informal language and recording, then mathematical language and symbols.

Reasoning

g) Present results in an organised way.
h) Understand a general statement and investigate whether particular cases match it.
i) Explain their methods and reasoning when solving problems involving number and data.

The lessons

Each lesson follows the same format.

Learning objectives
These are taken directly from the Yearly teaching programmes in the *Framework for Teaching Mathematics*. The solving problems objectives are linked with at least one other objective.

Vocabulary
This lists all the appropriate words and phrases to be used in the lesson. It is vital that children should see these words as well as hear them. So they should either be written on the board or, if sets of vocabulary cards are available, use these.

Resources
The lessons have been written to use a minimum of resources. Most of the resources listed would be found in most primary classrooms. Some lessons have resource sheets or activity sheets that can be photocopied. There are also three generic sheets on pages 78 to 80 that might prove useful for a variety of activities.

Oral and mental starter
These short sessions are intended to provide the children with a lively and fun start to the lesson. The objectives are taken from the National Numeracy Strategy's sample medium-term planning.

Teaching points
A detailed lesson plan to guide you through the lesson. The emphasis is on lively activities that will demonstrate to the children that mathematics is alive!

Plenary
All the plenaries have been planned to allow the children to reflect on what has gone before. Often there are 'challenges' included in the plenary. The principle here is to ensure that the children's ability is challenged but in a non-threatening way.

Support and Extension
These sections are aimed to support the less able and challenge the more able. The nature of problem solving is such that much of the work is 'open ended' and therefore differentiation should be more manageable.

Questions to guide assessment
Teacher assessment is an important component of teaching. These questions are included to help you focus on a small number of issues. The nature of problem solving is such that it is very difficult to make summative judgements. For example, 'Presents results in an organised way'. The child in Reception can do this in one way and a Y6 child in another way but both could be as valid. It is up to teachers to use their professional judgement through teacher assessment.

Calculators

Some of the lessons involve the use of calculators and in particular the OHP calculator. This is a very powerful learning tool for young children.

Wherever the calculator is suggested it is used to support children's learning. Therefore the approach in these books is in line with the recommendations of the National Numeracy Strategy.

Plan a feast

Framework for numeracy objectives

Solving problems: Problems involving 'real life', money and measures

- Solve word problems involving numbers in 'real life', money and measures, using one or more steps, including finding totals and giving change, and working out which coins to pay. Explain how the problem was solved.
- Recognise all coins and notes. Understand and use '£.p' notation (for example, know that £3.06 is £3 and 6p).

Calculations

- Extend understanding of the operations of addition and subtraction.
- Read and begin to write related vocabulary.
- Use '+', '–' and '=' signs.
- Recognise that addition can be done in any order.

VOCABULARY

altogether, total

Resources

- Photocopiable Sheets 1 and 2 (pages 42 and 43)
- Real or play coins
- OHP calculator

Oral and mental starter

Objective: Say the number that is 10 more or less, and the number that is 100 more or less, than any two-digit and three-digit number.

- Put the children into pairs. Enter a two-digit number into the OHP calculator. Ask one child in each pair to tell his or her partner which number is 10 greater than the number displayed. Ask a pair for the answer and then ask another pair to enter '+10' into the calculator. Who got the correct answer?
- Repeat this procedure with another two-digit number, but this time get the children to work out which number is 10 less than the displayed number.
- Repeat the procedure with three-digit numbers and 100 more, then 100 less.

Problem-solving challenge

Can you order a tasty meal for £15?

With the whole class

- Tell the children that they are going out for a meal at the world-famous Mega Bites café! You are such a kind teacher that you are going to give each of them £15.00 to spend on the meal. Ask them how much that is for each pair? Explain that you do not want them to have much change, so they have to spend as close to £15.00 as they can.

Children working in pairs

- Organise the children into pairs and give each pair copies of Photocopiable Sheets 1 and 2 (pages 42 and 43).
- They have to write down on Sheet 2 the following:
  - What they would choose;
  - How much it would cost;
  - What coins/notes they would use to pay for it;
  - How much change they would get.
- Stress that they need to check their calculations.

Plenary

- Ask the children questions such as:
  'How much did you spend, and what on?'

  'Did anyone spend exactly £15.00?

  'Did anyone have more than £1.00 change?'
- Ask further questions to discover what strategies they used to try to spend as near to £15.00 as possible, and how they checked their answers.
- Finish by giving the children this challenge:

  'Suppose I really did give you all £15.00 each. How much would that cost me?'

  The children can discuss in pairs how to solve this problem. Stress that you are not concerned with working out the answer, only with how to get the answer.
- Take feedback from the children and then try a few methods. If multiplication has not been mentioned, show how it can be used to solve the problem.

Support

- Limit the choices the children are allowed to make from the menu. For example, tell them that they are only allowed to choose three items – a main course, a dessert and a drink.
- How many different things could they choose between from each section, and how many altogether?

Extension

- Encourage the children to make choices from the menu so that they spend as close to £15.00 as possible. Challenge them to see who can get the closest to £15.00
- Ask the children to imagine that they could eat everything on the menu. How much would that cost – firstly, to order the food, and then in indigestion tablets or a weight-loss programme!

Questions to guide assessment

- What methods did the children use to add up the amounts?
- What methods did they use to calculate the change?
- Did they check their answers and, if so, what method did they use?

Money, money, money

Framework for numeracy objectives

Solving problems

- Solve word problems involving numbers in 'real life', money and measures, using one or more steps, including finding totals and giving change, and working out which coins to pay. Explain how the problem was solved.
- Recognise all coins and notes. Understand and use '£.p' notation (for example, know that £3.06 is £3 and 6p).

Calculations

- Use informal pencil-and-paper methods to support, record or explain hundreds, tens and units (HTU) +/– tens and units (TU), and HTU +/– HTU.
- Begin to use column addition and subtraction for HTU +/– TU where the calculation cannot easily be done mentally.
- Understand multiplication as repeated addition.

VOCABULARY

altogether, multiplication, repeated addition, total

Resources

- Large display coins
- Real or play coins
- Number fans
- Number lines
- Photocopiable Sheets 3 and 4 (pages 44 and 45)
- Whiteboards (optional)

Oral and mental starter

Objective: Recall addition and subtraction facts for each number up to at least 10.

- Give the children quickfire questions, such as:

  '5 + what equals 10?'
  '10 subtract 2 equals what?'

- The children can respond with number fans. In order to allow the less able some 'thinking time' for this activity, tell the children that when they have worked out the answer, they should hold the number fans close to their chest until you say, 'Fish and chips'. They then show their fans. The less able children would also benefit from access to a 1-to-10 number line.

Problem-solving challenge

How many coins make a pound?

With the whole class

- Write £1.00 on the board. Ask the children how many 50p coins you would need to pay for something that cost £1.00? Write '50p + 50p' on the board.
- Repeat this activity for 20p and 10p.
- Ask the children how many 2p coins would make £1.00? Ask a child to come out and write '2p + 2p', and so on on the board, but stop them after a short while and ask:

  'Who can think of a shorter way to write this information on the board?'

  Encourage the children to use multiplication as a way of recording, for example we can write '5 x 2p' instead of '2p + 2p + 2p + 2p + 2p'.

- Ask the children who can think of a way of paying for something that costs £1.00 using a mixture of coins. Encourage them to approach this in a logical way, for example all the ways that use 50p.
- Tell them that they are now going to solve similar problems for different amounts of money, this time recording them on some photocopiable sheets. Organise them into pairs or let them work individually if you prefer.

Children working individually or in pairs

- On a copy of photocopiable Sheet 3 (page 44), write in the top square an amount of money, such as £2, £5 or £10. Give each child or pair one of these sheets according to their ability. They have to draw in each box the exact number of coins shown in that box to make the total you have written.
- On Sheet 4 (page 45) you write an amount again at the top but this time there are no coins drawn in the boxes. The children have to choose a selection of coins to make that total. For example, if you have written £2 at the top, they could draw the following coins: £1, 50p, 20p, 10p, 10p, 5p, 2p, 2p, 1p.

Plenary

- Ask the children to tell you some of the amounts that they found and how they recorded them. Tell them that they are going to play 'Superquick Supermarket Shopping' or SSS, as it is known. They work in pairs with pencil and paper or whiteboards. Write £5.75 on the board and tell them that you have just bought something from a shop for £1.50 but you are not sure how much change you should have. The first pair to work this out has to put a finger on their noses! Ask them to explain how they got the correct answer.
- Repeat this for other amounts and vary the questions to cope with the range of ability in your class.

Support

- Enter suitable amounts on the photocopiable sheets for these children. They will probably need coins to help them calculate appropriate amounts and may require support in recording the answers appropriately. They will also need direct teaching in how to tackle the problems logically.

Extension

- Again, enter suitable amounts on the photocopiable sheets for these children to ensure they are sufficiently challenged. Try to ensure that they record using multiplication wherever possible.

Questions to guide assessment

- Did the children tackle the problems in a logical way?
- What methods of calculation did the children use?
- Did any child do everything mentally?
- Did children use column addition?
- Which children understood the concept of multiplication?

In search of Bigfoot

Framework for numeracy objectives

Solving problems

- Solve word problems involving numbers in 'measures', using one or more steps.

Measures

- Measure and compare using standard units (metres and centimetres).
- Begin to use decimal notation for metres and centimetres.

Handling data

- Solve a given problem by organising and interpreting numerical data in simple lists, tables and graphs.

VOCABULARY

line graph, longest, shortest, tallest

Resources

- A range of measuring equipment
- Photocopiable Sheets 5 and 6 (pages 46 and 47)

Oral and mental starter

Objective: Derive doubles of whole numbers up to 20 and the corresponding halves.

- Play 'Double and Halve it Bingo'. Ask the children to draw a 3 x 3 grid on a piece of paper. They have to write any nine numbers from 1 to 20 in each square. Call out various questions such as 'Double 6' and 'Half 18'. If the children have the answer written on their bingo card they can cross it off. You may like to throw in questions such as, 'Half 17' and ask the children why they could not have such a number on their card. The first child to complete a card wins the game.

Problem-solving challenge

Do tall people have the longest feet?

With the whole class

- Ask the children how many agree with this statement:

  'Tall people have longer feet than shorter people.'

  Take a vote amongst the class.
- Tell the children that they are going to investigate the statement. Throughout the lesson ensure that you and the children use the correct mathematical language and not words such as 'biggest' and 'largest', which could offend some children.
- Ask the children:

  'Who is the tallest in the class?'
- Follow this up by asking them to arrange themselves in order of height with, say, the tallest child at the front and the shortest at the back. You may need to leave the classroom to do this!
- Then ask:

  'Who has the longest feet?'
- Ask the children to see if they can get into line according to foot length, with the child with the longest feet at the front. This may lead to some confusion! Stop them and ask them to sit down. Explain that to find the answer to this question we will need to do some measuring.
- Talk to the children about how to measure the height of someone – which way you choose will depend on the measuring equipment you have – and then how to measure feet. For both these measurements the children should measure to the nearest centimetre. Show them how to record using decimal notation, for example 1.10m.

Children working in groups

- Divide the class into groups of about six. The children should take turns to measure each other's height and foot length. They can use photocopiable Sheet 5 (page 46) to record the results. Make sure that they record using appropriate decimal notation.
- When all the measurements have been completed, ask each group to write the two measurements for each child (but not the child's name) on the board.
- In order to prove the opening statement, plot the information on Sheet 6 (page 47). If you feel the children can do this themselves, give each group a copy of the sheet. The children can complete it in pairs, and this will help them check each other's work. If you feel that would be too difficult for them, then enlarge the sheet and stick it to the board or use it on an OHP or whiteboard. You can then plot the measurements for the whole class to see.

Plenary

- Discuss the results presented on the line graph and how to interpret this information. It should show a curve similar to the one below. Ask the children if it proves or disproves the statement.

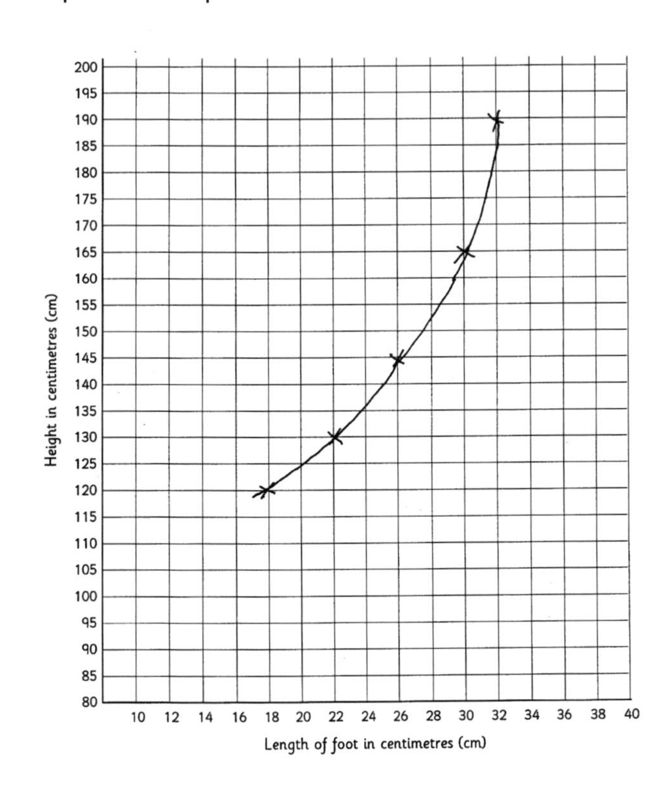

- Ask the children to get back into their groups and look for the length of their feet on the activity sheet. Tell them to remember that measurement.
- Then ask them to get into a line in order of foot length, with the shortest feet first. Once the children are in order, ask them to look at each other and see whether being in this line proves or disproves the statement.

Support

- For the actual measuring activity, there are two approaches you could adopt:
  - Put the less able children together in one group and either you or a classroom assistant has them as the focus group.
  - Put the children into mixed ability groups and encourage them to work together and help each other.

Extension

- An interesting way to extend this would be for a group of children to go around the school, measuring adults; in which case, it would be worthwhile telling staff that this was going to happen!

Questions to guide assessment

- Did the children cooperate with each other and work together?
- Could the children measure with reasonable accuracy?
- Could the children record with decimal notation?
- Could they plot the information on the line graph?

The time of your life

Framework for numeracy objectives

Solving problems: Making decisions

- Choose and use appropriate operations (including multiplication and division) to solve word problems, and appropriate ways of calculating: mental, mental with jottings, pencil and paper.

Measures

- Use a calendar.

Calculations

- Use knowledge that addition can be done in any order to do mental calculations more efficiently.
- Use informal pencil and paper methods to support, record or explain HTU +/– TU, HTU +/– HTU.
- Understand multiplication as repeated addition.

VOCABULARY

day, month, week, year

Resources

- Whiteboards
- Calculators
- Photocopiable Sheet 7 (page 48)

Oral and mental starter

Objective: Order a set of three-digit numbers.

- Ask a child to choose a digit from 1 to 9 and write it on the board. Repeat this with two other children to give a three-digit number. Repeat this until you have four three-digit numbers on the board. Tell the children they have to write these numbers on their whiteboards in order, from the smallest to largest.

- Repeat this.

Problem-solving challenge

How long have you been alive?

Whole class and in pairs

- Ask the children how old they are. They will probably respond in years only.

- Explain that today they will be finding out how old they are with a little more exactness! Ask a child how old he or she is and in which month he or she was born. Ask the children to recite the months of the year.

- Model on the board how to calculate ages in years and months.

- Let the children work in pairs to calculate their ages. They can use any method they want to calculate the answer.

- Go round the class, asking the children for their ages in years and months (for example, eight years and two months). In each case, ask in which month the child was born and encourage the rest of the class to check whether the given answer is correct.

- Then ask the children to calculate their ages in whole months only, again working in pairs (ie 98 months in the example above). Revise how many months there are in a year. Most children will just use addition (12 + 12 + 12, and so on), but some may realise that they can use multiplication to solve the problem. Ask them for their answers and how they calculated them. If they did not use multiplication, demonstrate how to do this on the board.

- Now explain that the age in months is not exact enough, so they are going to work out how long they have been alive in weeks! Ask the children how many weeks there are in a year. They work in pairs, using photocopiable Sheet 7 (page 48) to help them.

- Ask the children for their answers and how they calculated them. Try to find as many different calculation methods as you can.
- Explain that for the final challenge they are going to calculate how many **days** they have been alive. You will be able to stifle the moans by saying that those children who want to may use calculators. Be prepared for the issue of leap years to come up. The best way to cope with this is to say that, for the purposes of this activity, leap years don't exist. Again let them use Sheet 7 to help them.

Plenary

- Tell the children that the world record for standing on one leg is 71 hours! Ask them if they can calculate how many days and hours that would be? When they have worked this out, ask how they did it. Most of them will have added or perhaps multiplied lots of 24. Demonstrate on the board how they could have done this by division – taking away multiples of 24 until the number is below 24.
- Explain that the average adult spends 62 hours a week asleep. Ask the children to calculate how many hours a night that would be. When the children have worked this out, ask how they did it.

Support

- The most obvious way to support the children in this activity is to limit the degree of accuracy of their calculation. So that while the rest of the class is working on, say, the number of days, these children would be given additional time to complete the initial tasks of calculating the number of months or weeks.

Extension

- The more able children could miss out the initial activities and proceed straight to the more advanced calculations. They could also try to solve the days problem without using a calculator! They could even be asked to work out how long they have been alive in hours, then in minutes, and finally in seconds! They will probably realise that by the time they have worked out the final calculation, it will already have been rendered inaccurate by the passage of a few more seconds!
- Another challenge would be for them to work out how many days you have been alive – provided you are happy to admit your age, that is, and deal with additional greetings cards next birthday!

Questions to guide assessment

- Did the children use efficient methods to solve the problems?
- Did any child use multiplication to solve the problem, without any prompting?
- In the plenary, did any child use division to solve the problems?

Getting into shape

Framework for numeracy objectives

Solving problems: Reasoning about numbers or shapes

- Investigate a general statement about familiar numbers or shapes by finding examples that satisfy it.

Shape and space

- Make and describe shapes and patterns, for example explore the different shapes that can be made from four cubes.
- Relate solid shapes to pictures of them.

VOCABULARY

above, below, bottom, cube, different, over, same, side, top, under, underneath, vertex, vertices

Resources

- Set of 3D shapes
- Interlocking cubes
- Photocopiable Sheet 8 (page 49)

Oral and mental starter

Objective: Use mathematical vocabulary to name and describe some 3D shapes.

- Put a 3D shape in a bag so that the children cannot see it. Divide the class into two 'teams'. Each team has to take turns to ask questions to try to establish what the shape is.
- Encourage them to ask such questions as 'Does it have a curved side?' rather than to keep asking such questions as 'Is it a cube?'
- Repeat this for other shapes, perhaps choosing a child to come to the front to act as the teacher.

Problem-solving challenge

How many different ways can you join together four cubes?

With the whole class

- Explain to the children that today's challenge is to make as many different shapes as they can by joining together four cubes. Keep the introduction to this short because you want them to interpret this challenge for themselves. However, it would be worthwhile having some discussion on the meaning of 'same' and 'different'.
- Make up a shape, show it to the children and then rotate the shape. Ask the children if the shape is still the same or is it a different shape?

Children working individually/in pairs

- The children should then work individually to see how many different shapes they can make. There are eight possible shapes as shown below.

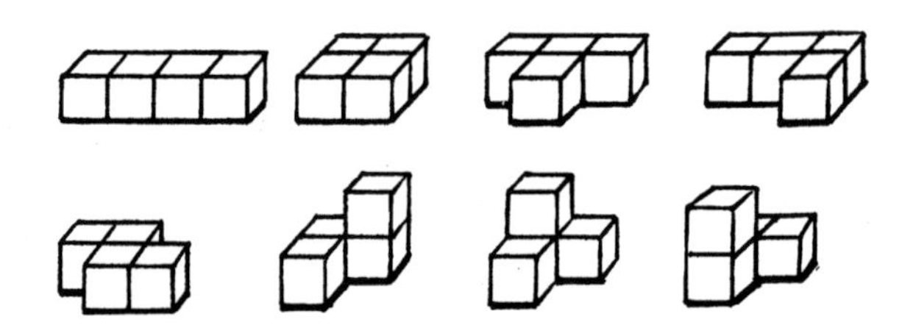

- When each child has found all eight ways, ask them to try and draw the shapes on photocopiable Sheet 8 (page 49). This will be very demanding and will take some time for them to do.
- When you have allowed enough time to make a good attempt at drawing the shapes, put the children into pairs. Explain that one child in each pair has to select one of the shapes that he or she made with four cubes, and ensure that the second child does not see it. The first child keeps the shape

hidden under the table and describes it to the second child, who then has to make that shape but not let the first child see what is being made. Remind them that the colour of the cubes is not important.

- When the second child thinks that he or she has made the shape, both children reveal their shapes. They then swap roles and try again with a different shape.

Plenary

- Ask a child to choose one of the shapes he or she made and describe it to the rest of the class to see if they can make it.
- If a child has been making shapes with five cubes (see Extension below), ask him or her to describe the shape for the rest of the class to make. Alternatively, you can make and describe a shape using five cubes.

Support

- Most Year 3 children should be able to find at least **some** of the possible shapes with four cubes. However, if this proves difficult for some, the task could be simplified to finding as many shapes as they can with three cubes.

Extension

- A useful extension of this activity would be for the children to find as many shapes as they can with five cubes.

Questions to guide assessment

- Did the children tackle the problem in a systematic way?
- Did the children use the correct mathematical language in describing their shapes?
- Could the children represent their shapes on paper?

Lines of symmetry

Framework for numeracy objectives

Solving problems; Reasoning about numbers or shapes

- Solve mathematical problems or puzzles, recognise simple patterns and relationships, generalise and predict. Suggest extensions by asking 'What if...?'

Shape and space

- Identify and sketch lines of symmetry in simple shapes, and recognise shapes with no lines of symmetry.
- Sketch the reflection of a simple shape in a mirror line along one edge.

VOCABULARY

line of symmetry, mirror line, reflection, symmetrical

Resources

- Whiteboards
- Mirrors
- Felt-tipped pens or pencil crayons
- 2D shapes or photocopiable Sheets 9 and 10 (pages 50 and 51)

Oral and mental starter

Objective: Recall multiplication facts in 2x, 4x, 5x, and 10x tables.

- Ask the children to recite the 2x table. As they do, write the answers on the board.
- Now tell them that they have to work out the 4x table by doubling the answers to the 2x table and write the answers on their whiteboards. When they have finished, ask them to call out the answers and write these on the board.
- Point to 16 and ask the children how many times 4 this is. Repeat this with other answers.
- Ask the children to recite the 10x table and write the answers on the board.
- Ask them to write the answers to the 5x table on their whiteboards by halving the answers to the 10x table.

Problem-solving challenge

How many lines of symmetry does a shape have?

With the whole class

- Ask the children to tell you what they know about symmetry. When they have done this, ask them to look around the classroom for a few moments and then tell you some things in the room that are symmetrical.
- Explain that today's challenge is to find lines of symmetry in different shapes.

Children working in pairs

- Group the children in pairs. Give each pair a copy of photocopiable Sheet 9 (page 50). Using the square shapes only at this stage, or your own range of 2D squares, tell them that they are to use them to make shapes. The finished shapes have to be in two groups:
  a) those with lines of symmetry;
  b) those without any lines of symmetry.
- Ask the children if they think that they can make any shapes in group b.
- They should sketch their shapes on paper and mark on the lines of symmetry. Remind them that they can check their lines of symmetry by using a mirror. Some examples of what they might do are shown at the top of the next page.

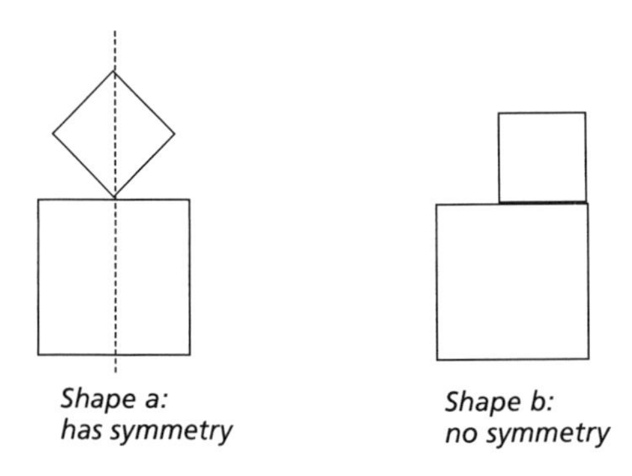

Shape a: has symmetry   *Shape b: no symmetry*

- When the children have completed this activity, they can do the same activity using the triangles. Tell the children that they have to choose one of their shapes to show the rest of the class in the plenary session.
- Now give the children copies of Sheet 10 (page 51) or four rectangles of different sizes. The challenge is to use all four rectangles to make a shape that has as many lines of symmetry as they can find. Tell them to mark each line of symmetry in a different colour. Possible examples are shown below.

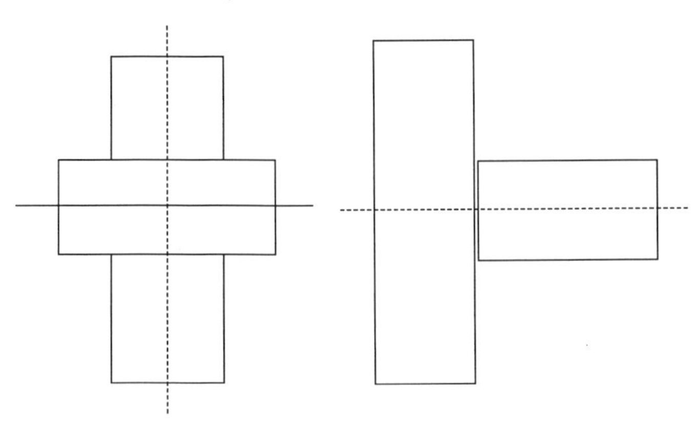

Plenary

- Choose some children to bring out their shapes and, in each case, to sketch just half of the shape on the board. (You could do this for them if necessary.) The rest of the class has to sketch the complete shape on a piece of paper and show you the results. Repeat this for a number of different shapes.
- Ask the children if anyone found a shape that did not have any lines of symmetry. If so, ask them to sketch this shape on the board. Then discuss with the class whether they agree that there are no lines of symmetry or if anyone can see any lines of symmetry.
- Finally, ask the children how many lines of symmetry they found with the rectangle shape.

Support

- Rather than move the children on to the rectangle challenge, let them continue working on the first challenge.

Extension

- Rather than giving these children the first challenge, it would be appropriate to set them the second challenge straightaway.
- A further extension activity would be to let the children use combinations of different shapes and to find lines of symmetry in these.

Questions to guide assessment

- Were the children confident in finding lines of symmetry?
- Could the children use the correct mathematical language in describing the shape?
- Did the children need to use mirrors to find the lines of symmetry?

Another brick in the wall

Framework for numeracy objectives

Solving problems: Reasoning about numbers or shapes

- Solve mathematical problems or puzzles, recognise simple patterns and relationships, generalise and predict. Suggest extensions by asking 'What if...?'

Calculations

- Use knowledge that addition can be done in any order to do mental calculations more efficiently.
- Use known number facts and place value to add/subtract mentally.

VOCABULARY

add, addition, count on, minus, subtract, subtraction

Resources

- Whiteboards
- Number lines
- 100 squares
- Cubes
- Activity sheets 11 and 12 (pages 52 and 53)

Oral and mental starter

Objective: State subtraction facts corresponding to addition facts, and vice versa.

- Write on the board an addition sentence, such as: 7 + 2 = 9. The children work in pairs with whiteboards and write down two subtraction sentences using these numbers.
- Once the children have demonstrated that they understand the idea, move on to more challenging numbers, for example 376 + 234 = 610.

Problem-solving challenge

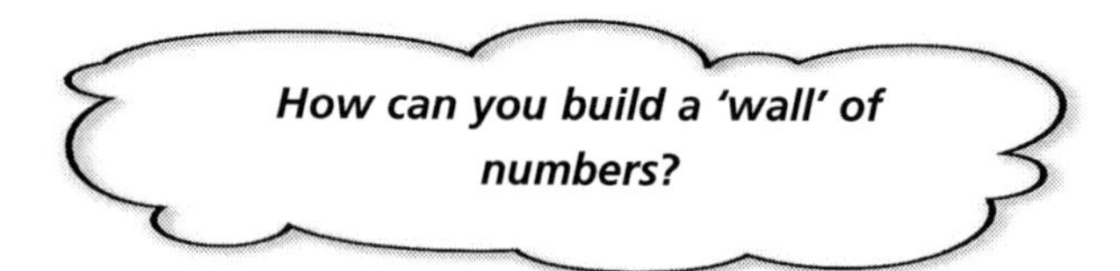

Whole class and individuals/pairs

- Draw the following 'wall' on the board.

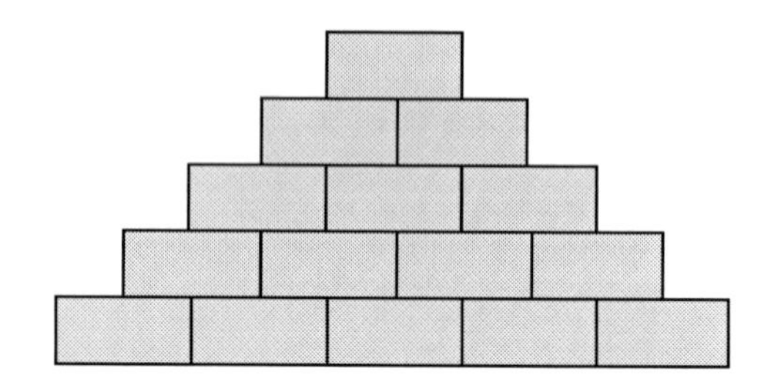

- Explain to the children that this is called a 'number wall'. First, you have to insert numbers into the bottom row of bricks. Then, to find the number in a brick in the rows above, you have to add together the numbers in the two bricks immediately beneath. Show them how to do this, reminding them of the strategy of adding the biggest number first.
- Ask the children to help you add all the bricks up until you get to the top brick. If the calculations are too difficult for the children, let them use paper and pencil. Encourage them to use jottings to work out the answer – they could use an empty number line or partitioning.
- Working individually or in pairs, give the children copies of photocopiable Sheet 11 (page 52). Explain that the challenge is to arrange the digits 1 to 5 in the bottom row of bricks in such a way as to get the highest number possible in the top brick. Stress to them that no digit may be used more than once in the bottom row of each wall.

The highest number possible is 61, as follows:

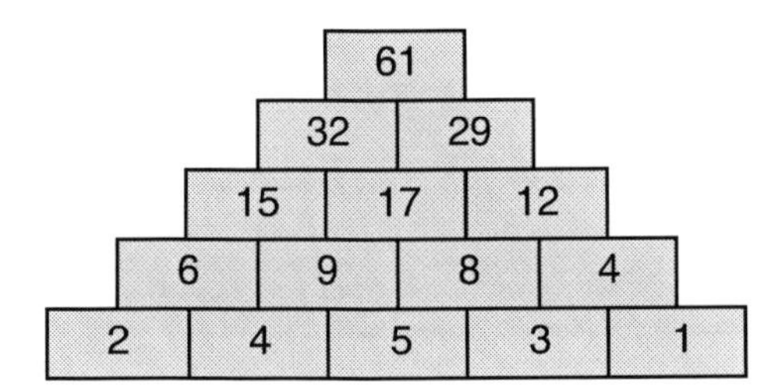

If any children suggest a larger number, you can tell instantly that they will need to check their addition. The order for the bottom row in this case is 2, 4, 5, 3, 1. There are other solutions. The basic strategy is to put the largest number in the centre brick, followed by the next largest in the adjacent bricks, and so on.

- Discuss this strategy with the children and then set the task of finding the lowest total possible (35), as follows:

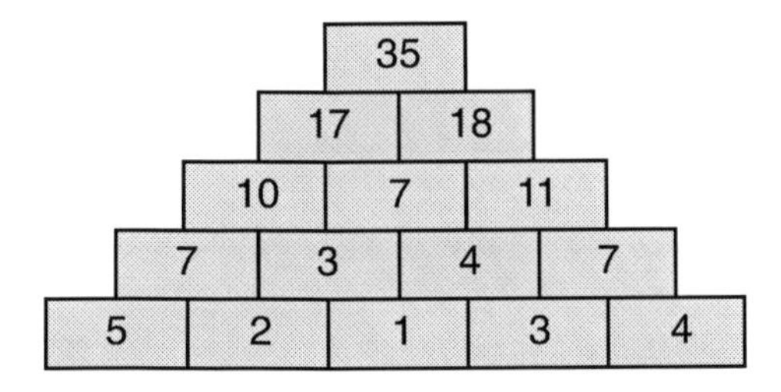

Some children may use the correct strategy straightaway, but this would be unusual.

- When the children have found the lowest total, refer back to the blank wall on the board. Write 25 in the top brick and ask the children to suggest pairs of numbers that add up to 25. Ask what strategy they used to work this out. They may have counted on or used subtraction.
- Write a suitable pair of numbers (8 and 17, say) in the two bricks below the top one. Keep going down the wall until you get to a number that can only be split into a fraction or decimal (as with the activity above, the rule is that any given number may only feature in the bottom row of the wall once). Explain that the challenge is to find a number to go in the top brick that can be subtracted all the way down the wall, without getting into fractions or decimals.

Plenary

- Ask the children to give you examples of numbers that have 'made it' to the bottom row. Write the numbers on the board and encourage the rest of the class to check the calculations.
- Ask for a number that did not 'make it' to the bottom row and write it on the board. See if the children can use fractions to get to the bottom row.

Support

- To support the less able children, give them the same problem but using Activity sheet 12 (page 53). This uses only the digits 1 to 4. Make sure that they have adequate resource support to help them calculate, such as number lines, hundred squares and cubes.

Extension

- Once the children have found one answer to the 'subtraction wall', ask them to find as many different answers as they can with the same number in the top brick.

Questions to guide assessment

- Could the children transfer skills from one problem to another?
- Did the children use efficient methods of calculation?
- Did the children persevere with the problems?

Playing the triangle

Framework for numeracy objectives

Solving problems: Reasoning about numbers or shapes

- Solve mathematical problems or puzzles, recognise simple patterns and relationships, generalise and predict. Suggest extensions by asking 'What if...?'

Calculations

- Use knowledge that addition can be done in any order to do mental calculations more efficiently.
- Use known number facts and place value to add mentally.

VOCABULARY

add, addition, triangle

Resources

- Number lines, number squares and number cards
- Cubes
- Whiteboards
- Photocopiable Sheet 13 (page 54)

Oral and mental starter

Objectives: Read and write whole numbers to 1000. Say numbers that are 10 or 100 more or less than any given three-digit number.

- On their whiteboards or paper ask the children to draw three boxes to represent HTU.
- Using number cards from 1 to 9, shuffle the cards and draw one out at random. The children have to decide to write that number in the H, T or U box. The aim is that, when all three boxes have digits in them, the number is as high as possible.
- Repeat this for the next two boxes and then ask a child to read out the number. Make sure they say the number and don't just read out the digits, for example 'Three hundred and twenty one' rather than '3, 2, 1.'

Problem-solving challenge

What is the largest total, and what is the smallest total, you can get from a 'number' triangle?

With the whole class

- Draw the following triangle on the board.

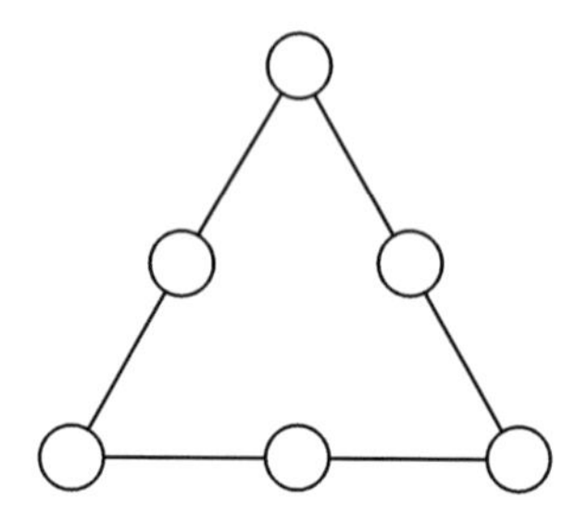

- Put the digits 1 to 6 into the circles. Explain to the children how to add up the sides of the triangle to get a total like this:

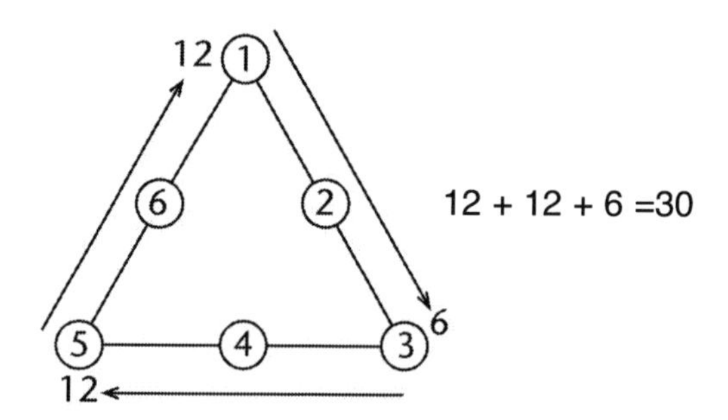

- Tell the children that today's challenge is to arrange the digits 1 to 6 in such a way that when we add the sides we get the highest total possible. To help them record this, give them photocopiable Sheet 13 (page 54). Give the children time to find the highest total possible (36). Some children will be able to calculate mentally while others will need to use jottings.

- When the children have found the highest total, demonstrate the solution on the board, as follows:

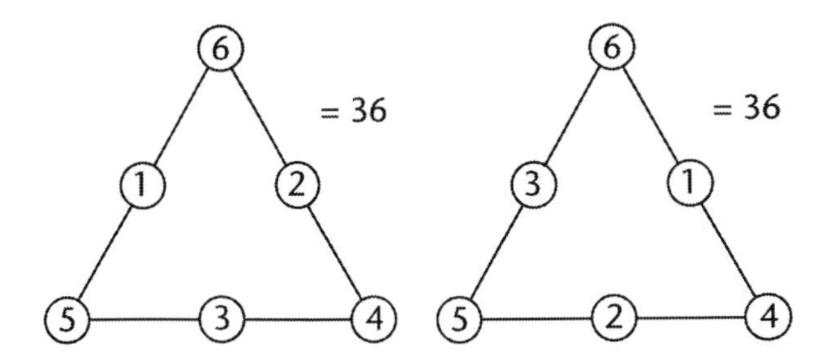

The strategy for finding the solution is to place the largest numbers (i.e. 4, 5 and 6) in the corner circles, where they will be added twice.

- Set the children the challenge of finding the lowest total possible (27). Some children may transfer the strategy for finding the highest to this problem, though, in reality, few do. When they have found the lowest total, demonstrate on the board how this must be the lowest.

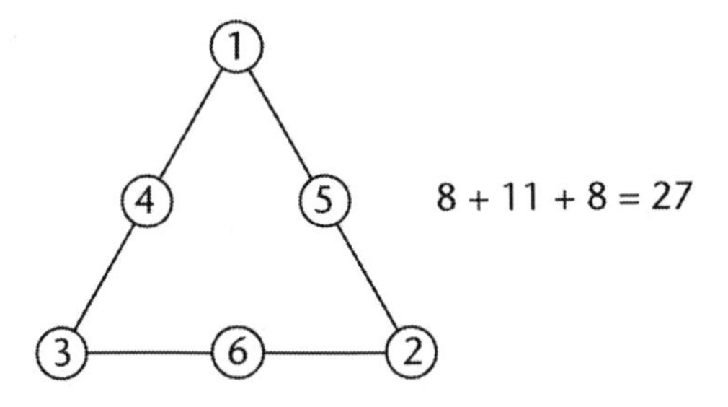

- Now set the children the challenge of finding all the possible totals from 27 to 36.

Plenary

- Ask the children to read out how they worked out all the totals from 28 to 35. For each total, ask which children did it the same way and which used a different way.
- Refer back to the first problem. Ask the children if anyone could predict what the total would be if the numbers were 10, 20, 30, 40, 50 and 60. If no child can, show them the link between the two answers. Then write up 100, 200, 300, 400, 500 and 600, and ask the children to predict the answer this time.

Support

- Most Year 3 children should be able to cope with the concept of this problem but may have problems with the addition. Provide them with appropriate resources to aid their calculations – number lines, number squares, cubes and so on.

Extension

- Challenge the children to use six other consecutive numbers of their choice (11 to 16, say) and investigate the highest and lowest totals. Encourage them to do the calculations mentally.

Questions to guide assessment

- Could the children transfer skills from one problem to another?
- Did the children use efficient methods of calculation?
- Did the children persevere with the problems?

What's the difference?

Framework for numeracy objectives

Solving problems: Reasoning about numbers or shapes

- Solve mathematical problems or puzzles, recognise simple patterns and relationships, generalise and predict. Suggest extensions by asking 'What if...?'

Calculations

- Use knowledge that addition can be done in any order to do mental calculations more efficiently.
- Use known number facts and place value to add/subtract mentally.
- Find a small difference by counting up from the smaller to the larger number.

VOCABULARY

addition, difference, even, odd, subtraction, total

Resources

- OHP calculator
- Whiteboards
- Resource sheet 14 (page 55)

Oral and mental starter

Objective: Count in threes from and back to zero.

- Set the OHP calculator to go up in threes: 3 + = =. Tell the children that this calculator is going to count up in threes. Press the equals key repeatedly.
- Reset the calculator and say that this time the children have to shout out the next number before you press the equals key. Keep pressing the equals key slowly until the number is too big for the children to handle.
- Enter '30 – 3 =' into the calculator. Press the equals key repeatedly and the calculator will count down. Reset the calculator and again ask the children to shout out the answers before the calculator displays them. Make sure you go into negative numbers.
- Repeat this with other 'start' numbers within the children's ability level.

Problem-solving challenge

Can you solve all these problems?

With the whole class

- This lesson is based on using photocopiable Sheet 14 (page 55) and setting the children short mental challenges. Either enlarge Sheet 14 to A3 size so that it can be stuck on the board or give the children individual copies of it.
- Tell the children that you are going to set them lots of short challenges, which they can work on in pairs. They are to do them mentally, but they may use jottings if they wish. Provide paper or whiteboards for the recording.

Children working in pairs

- Organise the class into pairs and tell the children that they may work out the answers to their questions together with their partners. Set them the challenges one at a time and tell them to work out the answer, but not to put their hands up or shout out!

The challenges

1) Which two numbers when added have the highest total? (108 + 103 = 211)
2) Which two numbers have the lowest total? (75 + 82 = 157)

3) Which three numbers when added have the highest total? (108 + 103 + 101 = 312)
4) Find three pairs of numbers that add together to give the answer as an even number. (**Note:** there are more than three possible answers.)
5) Which two numbers have the largest difference? (108 – 75)
6) Which two numbers have the smallest difference? (84 – 82)
7) Find three pairs of numbers where the difference is an odd number. (**Note:** there are more than three possible answers.)
8) Find three numbers that have a difference of 5 between them? (91/96/101)
9) When I made one number five times bigger, the answer was 505. What was the number? (101)
10) When I made a number five times bigger, the answer was 375. What was the number? (75)

- After an appropriate length of time, select children to give you the answers. Ask the children how they arrived at their answer and what strategies they used. Make the lesson lively and fun by rewarding the children. Give them stickers, applaud them! Say they don't have to come to school on Saturday!
- Now give the children some time to make up questions of their own. The questions must involve addition and subtraction.

Plenary

- Ask children to tell you the questions they thought up and ask the rest of the class to work them out. Correct any misconceptions or errors in the questions.
- As a final challenge, ask:

  What's the total of all the numbers?

  Obviously, the children will need to write something down to solve this (the answer is 829).
- In the case of lower-achievers, ask them to add a row or a column.

Support

- With the whole class working together in this, support should be given by providing the children resources to help them – number lines, 100 squares, and so on.
- You could also make these children the target group. This would enable you to give the children 'extra' time to work out some of the problems.

Extension

- Encourage the children to perform all the calculations mentally and to do them quickly. In the case of the questions that ask for three answers, ask the children for more answers!

Questions to guide assessment

- Did the children tackle the problems in a systematic way?
- Did the children use jottings or calculate mentally?
- Did their problems demonstrate a good understanding of addition and subtraction?

Growing up?

Framework for numeracy objectives

Solving problems: Problems involving 'real life', money and measures

- Use all four operations to solve word problems involving numbers in 'real life' and measures, using one or more steps, including converting metres to centimetres and vice versa.

Calculations

- Develop and refine written methods for column addition and subtraction of two whole numbers less than 1000, and addition of more than two such numbers.
- Use known number facts and place value to add or subtract mentally, including any pair of two-digit whole numbers.

Measures

- Use, read and write standard metric units (metre, centimetre, millimetre), including their abbreviations (m, cm, mm).
- Suggest suitable units and measuring equipment to estimate or measure length.

VOCABULARY

centimetre, estimate, metre, millimetre

Resources

- Measuring equipment
- Metre sticks
- Centimetre rulers
- Tape measures of different lengths
- Calculators
- Activity sheet 15 (page 56)

Oral and mental starter

Objective: Derive addition pairs that total 100.

- Tell the children they have 10 minutes to write down pairs of numbers that add together to make 100 (for example, 43 + 57; 9 + 91). They should try to write as many pairs as possible. Remind them of the need to adopt a logical approach to this activity.
- When the time is up, ask the children how many pairs they found. Ask them what strategies they used to try and get as many pairs as possible.

Problem-solving challenge

Are the oldest people also the tallest?

With the whole class

- Explain that today's challenge is to find who will be the tallest person in the class when all the children have reached the age of 65! The first activity is to find out how tall everyone is. Ask the class to get into a straight line in height order, shortest first. Try to give the children minimum help in this activity as they **should** be able to do it by themselves. Tell the class that this height order is the order in which they are to go into assembly for the week, though you might want to vary it and have the tallest go first.

Children working in groups/pairs

- Divide the class into groups and give each group some measuring equipment. Give them photocopiable Sheet 15 (page 56) and ask them to write in the names of the people in their group. They then have to write their estimates of each person's height in two ways: firstly, in metres and centimetres and, secondly, in centimetres only.

- When they have done this, ask some children for their estimates and how they have written them (1.20m or 1m 20cm). Neither is incorrect but the decimal way of recording is a good lead into the concept of decimals.
- Now let the children do the measuring – give them freedom to measure how they want, for now.
- When they have entered the measurements on Sheet 15, give them some time to calculate the difference between their estimates and the actual measurement.
- Ask them what their closest estimate was: did anyone get the estimate exactly right?
- Talk to the children about how we actually stop growing at the age of about 17 to 18 and that in real life older people can actually shrink! Tell them that they are going to have a bit of fun with the challenge by pretending that people keep growing until they are 65! To do this, we are going to give different groups 'growing rates'. Allocate each group a 'growth rate' of between 8cm and 14cm a year.
- Let the children work in pairs to calculate how tall each child would be at the age of 65. Let them choose which method of calculation to use. They need to calculate how many years it will take to reach 65, how many centimetres that would be in total, and then the actual height at 65! Encourage them to check their work, using calculators if appropriate.

Plenary

- Ask the children to read out their projected heights. There would be some very tall people around! To give the children an idea of how tall some of them would be if they kept on growing, ask a child to measure out the distance on the floor or in the corridor.
- Finish the lesson with a discussion and perhaps ask the children to imagine the heights and lengths involved in these amazing facts:
  - Tallest living women – 2.31m
  - Tallest living man – 2.35m
  - Longest human hair length – 5.15m

Support

- Give the children a 'growth rate' that they can easily calculate with, such as 10cm per year. Alternatively, ask them to estimate the height for a younger age – 20, for example.

Extension

- Give these children a really challenging 'growth rate', such as 10.23cm per year. They could also be given a longer time period, for example to estimate how tall they would be if they lived to be 99?
- Encourage them to choose an appropriate calculation method, such as multiplication.

Questions to guide assessment

- Did the children cooperate and work together?
- Did the children choose appropriate measuring equipment?
- Did the children choose the appropriate means of calculation?

Adventure Island

Framework for numeracy objectives

Solving problems: Problems involving 'real life', money and measures

- Use all four operations to solve word problems involving numbers in 'real life', money and measures (including time), using one or more steps, including converting pounds to pence and vice versa.

Calculations

- Use informal pencil and paper methods to support, record or explain additions/subtractions.
- Develop and refine written methods for column addition and subtraction of two whole numbers less than 1,000, and addition of more than two such numbers.
- Money calculations (for example, £7.85 ± £3.49).
- Extend understanding of the operations of multiplication and division, and their relationship to each other and to addition and subtraction.

Measures

- Use, read and write the vocabulary related to time.
- Estimate/check times using minutes and hours.

VOCABULARY

Altogether, total

Resources

- Whiteboards
- Photocopiable Sheets 16 to 19 (pages 57 to 60)

Oral and mental starter

Objective: Begin to recall facts in the 6x and 8x tables.

- Ask the children to say the 3x table and write the answers on the board. Now ask them to write on their whiteboards the double of each number. Ask such questions as 'What would 4 x 6 be?'
- Repeat this for the 4x table, and then the 8x table.

Is it possible to have three days of fun and still have change from £50?

With the whole class

Problem-solving challenge

- Explain to the children that they are going to plan an adventure holiday. Show them photocopiable Sheet 16 (page 57), either enlarged to A3 or allocate each pair a copy. The sheet shows the cost of activities on Adventure Island. The island provides activities for two hours in the morning and two hours in the afternoon. The children will be there for three days. Each child has £50.00 to spend on the activities. They have to plan which activities they are going to do, the rule being they must try all the activities at least once. They have to calculate the total cost and any change from £50.00 they may have. They can use Sheet 19 (page 60) to record their 'timetable' and its cost.

Children working in pairs

- The children should tackle the task in pairs, sharing a copy of Sheet 16 and completing Sheet 19.
- Have some questions prepared for those children who finish early, for example:

- ***If eight children went rock climbing, how much would that cost in total?***
- ***If seven children went pony trekking, how much would that cost in total?***
- ***A number of children went abseiling and the total cost was £42.75. How many children went?***
- ***A number of children went canoeing and the total cost was £53.90. How many children went?***

- ***Two children went on the same two activities and the cost was £13.40. Which two activities might they have been?***

Plenary

- Ask the children for the amount of change each pair had. Which pair had the lowest amount? Give the children this problem to solve:

  If there was a class of 30 children and they each had £50 to spend, how much would that be altogether?

  Ask for the answer and the ways the children worked out the answer. Model some of those ways on the board – make sure that multiplication is one of them.

- Tell the children that the price for adults is twice the cost of the children's price. Ask them to work out the cost of the activities for adults as quickly as they can.

Support

- Give these children a copy of Sheet 17 (page 58), which has easier calculations on it for the children to do. Do not give them a spending limit.

Extension

- Give these children Sheet 18 (page 59), which has more difficult calculations. Keep the same £50 spending limit.
- The children could also be asked to make up their own questions like those above.

Questions to guide assessment

- Did the children tackle the problem in a logical way?
- What types of informal written methods did the children use?
- Did the fact that the problems were relating to money confuse the children?

On the shelf

Framework for numeracy objectives

Solving problems: Problems involving 'real life', money and measures

- Use all four operations to solve word problems involving numbers in 'real life'.

Calculations

- Approximate first. Use informal pencil and paper methods to support, record or explain multiplications and divisions.
- Develop and refine written methods for column addition of two whole numbers less than 1,000, and addition of more than two such numbers.
- Check with the inverse operation.

VOCABULARY

approximate, average, division, estimate, multiplication

Resources

- Number fans or whiteboards
- A range of reading books

Oral and mental starter

Objective: Multiply tens and units by units.

- Give the children some 'quickfire' questions, such as 20 x 3, 31 x 9, 25 x 4 and 99 x 8. They can respond with either number fans or whiteboards. Vary the questions to cover the range of ability within the class or target certain groups with specific questions.

Problem-solving challenge

How many words are there in a book?

With the whole class

- This challenge involves words and books. Before the lesson, collect a selection of books of different lengths. Show the children a book with very few pictures in it or, even better, none at all. Ask 'How many words do you think are in this book?' Write a few of their, no doubt, wild guesses on the board.
- Ask how they think we could find out how many words there are. While the response 'Count them' is a possible solution, that could take some time! So ask for ways in which we could approximate the number of words. If they don't suggest the following process, go through it with them:
  - First, count the number of words on one full page (X).
  - Then count the pages or use the page numbers to work out how many pages (Y)
  - Multiply X by Y.
- Demonstrate the process using the book you showed the children earlier. Ask one child to count the words on a page. If you have another copy of the same book, another child could be working out the number of pages. Choose a book with as many pages in as you think the children can cope with mathematically. If the numbers are 'awkward', talk about 'rounding up and down'. Then round the numbers and write them on the board.
- Ask the children what you need to do with the numbers to solve this problem. If they don't suggest multiplication, then demonstrate how to do this by an informal method. Ask them to approximate the answer first. If the number of words on the page was, say, 120 and the number of pages was 40, the 120 could be divided into two separate multiplications, as follows: 100 x 40 and 20 x 40.

- Ask the children how they could check that the answer is correct. Demonstrate how to check by division if that is appropriate.

Children working in pairs

- Tell the children that now they are going to do the same activity in pairs. Say you would like them to find the answer by multiplication, if possible.
- After they have found the answer for two books get the class together for a 'mini-plenary'. Explain that this method of finding the number of words in a book is alright, but we could try to be more exact. Ask them if they can think of ways to get an answer that is more exact.
- Demonstrate that one way would be to count, say, three pages and then divide the answer by three. Do this on the board referring to a real book. While the concept of the average is a Year 6 objective, this activity is a good introduction to the term and, also, does provide good practice in a real context of division. Let the children try to refine their answers.
- There could be many variations on this idea of counting words in books, depending on the ability and interest of the children. These include:
  - the number of sentences on a page and therefore in the book;
  - the number of chapters in, say, three books;
  - choosing a particular word (for example 'and') and counting the number of times it occurs on a single page and then estimating how many times that it would occur in the book.

Plenary

- Talk to the children about the process of counting words and how sometimes they may, in the future, have to write something that is, for example, no more than 500 words, at high school perhaps. Fortunately, if the writing is done on a computer, the computer does it for us!
- If the classroom has a bookcase refer to that; if not ask the children to imagine a bookcase full of books. Ask them how we could roughly work out how many books there are on the bookcase.
- Finish by asking the children to think about how we would find out:
  - how many books there are in the school library;
  - how many books there are in the local library;
  - how many books there are in the whole of the country;
  - how many books there are in the whole wide world.

Support

- For the main teaching activity, choose a book that has both a words total and number of pages that are within the children's mathematical ability.

Extension

- For the main teaching activity, choose a book that has both the words total and number of pages that will stretch the children's mathematical ability.
- Alternatively, use some of the ideas suggested above.

Questions to guide assessment

- Did the children cooperate in the activity?
- Which children used multiplication as a method?
- Did the children use appropriate checking strategies?

Multiplication and division

Framework for numeracy objectives

Solving problems

- Choose and use appropriate number operations and appropriate ways of calculating (mental, mental with jottings, pencil and paper) to solve problems.

Calculations

- Approximate first. Use informal pencil and paper methods to support, record or explain multiplications and divisions.
- Use known number facts and place value to add or subtract mentally, including any pair of two-digit whole numbers.
- Extend understanding of the operations of multiplication and division, and their relationship to each other and to addition and subtraction.

VOCABULARY

division, inverse, multiplication

Resources

- Whiteboards
- Photocopiable Sheets 20 to 22 (pages 61 to 63)

Oral and mental starter

Objective: Recall addition and subtraction facts for each number to 20.

- Write a number between 1 and 20 on the board. Ask the children to write down an addition and subtraction sum that uses the number on the board either as the answer or as part of the sum. Repeat this with other numbers.

Problem-solving challenge

How many ways are there to connect two numbers?

With the whole class

- Write on the board:
  = 8

  Tell the children that you want them to think of a calculation that would equal 8. The answer will probably be an addition. Ask them to give you a subtraction, multiplication and division sum that equals 8. Write the answers you get on the board.

Working in pairs

- Organise the children into pairs. Then write on the board:
  = 28

  Ask the children to talk to their partner and try to think of a calculation for each operation where the answer is 28. Tell them to think of the hardest calculations they can! Write the answers on the board.

- Now write on the board:
  10 □ □ = 20

  Ask the children to think of an operation and a number that would make the calculation correct (for example 'x 2' or '+ 10'). When they suggest an addition and multiplication solution, stress the links between the two operations.

- Now write on the board:
  50 □ □ = 25

  Ask the children to come up with two answers to make this calculation correct. Again stress the links between division and subtraction.

- Hand out photocopiable Sheet 20 (page 61). Let the children choose their own calculation methods to complete the challenges. The answers are:

Clouds A and B

99 → 120	+21
51 → 72	+21
18 → 39	+21
26 → 7	–19
100 → 81	–19
7 → 35	x5
15 → 75	x5
63 → 21	÷3
99 → 33	÷3
60 → 20	÷3

Clouds C and D

There are two ways to link each number in cloud C to the numbers in cloud D. The answers are:

90 = 99 – 9 and 30 x 3

88 = 72 + 16 and 97 – 9

48 = 32 + 16 and 16 x 3

23 = 32 – 9 and 92 ÷ 4

21 = 84 ÷ 4 and 7 x 3

- When the children have finished these challenges, give them a copy of photocopiable Sheet 21 (page 62). This is blank for them to devise their own challenges. You can either let them choose the link operations and numbers or you can specify what they are.

Plenary

- Ask the children for two single-digit even numbers and two two-digit even numbers and write them on the board. With the children working in pairs, ask them if they can use all four operations to link the numbers on the board.

Support

- Use blank Sheet 21 (page 62) to set appropriate challenges for these children.

Extension

- Use blank Sheet 21 to set appropriate challenges for these children.
- Use Sheet 22 (page 63). The answers are:

26	x 2	52	–50	2
88	+ 33	121	-99	22
20	x 5	100	÷100	1
13	x 3	39	–10	29
60	x 4	240	÷ 4	60
17	+ 58	75	÷5	15
98	x 2	196	–99	97
52	+ 48	100	÷4	25

- The second part of the sheet is blank for the children to make up their own problems. You could use this to show the importance of inverse operations. for example, 26 x 2 = 52 – 52 ÷ 2 = 26.

Questions to guide assessment

- Did the children persevere with the problems?
- Which children used mental methods?
- Which children used informal written methods?

Staying in shape

Framework for numeracy objectives

Solving problems: Reasoning about numbers and shapes

- Solve mathematical problems or puzzles, recognise and explain patterns and relationships, generalise and predict. Suggest extensions by asking 'What if...?'

Shape and space

- Make shapes: for example, construct polygons and discuss properties such as lines of symmetry.
- Recognise equilateral and isosceles triangles.
- Classify polygons using criteria such as number of angles, whether or not they are regular, and symmetry properties.

VOCABULARY

angle, equilateral, irregular, isosceles, line of symmetry, regular

Resources

- Photocopiable Sheets 23 to 25 (pages 64 to 66)

Oral and mental starter

Objective: To visualise 2D shapes.

- The children will need pencils and paper. Give them the following instructions:

  'Close your eyes and imagine a triangle, any kind of triangle. Now imagine another triangle exactly the same as the first one. Put the two triangles together to make a regular shape. Open your eyes and draw the shape that you made.'

- When they have drawn their shapes, ask them to talk to each other about the shapes. Ask them to hold up their shapes for you to see. Were any of the shapes the same? Did anyone not draw a regular shape?

Problem-solving challenge

How many sides does a shape have?

With the whole class

- Either draw a large equilateral triangle on the board or use the template on photocopiable Sheet 23 (page 65). Ask the children questions about the properties of the triangle, such as:

  'What is this type of triangle called?'

  'How many sides has it got?'

  'How many angles has it got?'

  'How many lines of symmetry does it have?'

  'Is it a regular or irregular shape, and why?'

- Then ask the same questions about the isosceles triangle (using photocopiable Sheet 24).
- Explain that the challenge is to use triangles to make other shapes. Give out copies of Sheet 23 and ask the children to cut out the triangles. Using the two equilateral triangles (every time you say 'equilateral', ask the children what makes a triangle equilateral – this constant reinforcement of the terms should help them to remember them), demonstrate how to make other shapes by either joining the shapes together or overlapping them. Let the children experiment with this idea for a while before giving them the following challenge.
- Give out copies of Sheets 23 and 25. Explain that the challenge is to use Sheet 23 to make as many different shapes as possible with the two triangles, and also to try and make a shape with as many sides as possible. Explain that on Sheet 25 they have to sketch the shapes they have made, write their names (if they can), say how many sides and angles they have, whether they have any lines of symmetry and whether or not they are regular shapes.

- When most of the children have completed the sheet, stop them and ask them questions about the shapes they have made, for example:

  'Has anyone made a shape with 120 sides!'

  'Has anyone made a shape with 10 sides?'

  'If it has 10 sides, how many angles has it got?'

- Give out Sheet 24. Ask the children what is special about an isosceles triangle. Ask them to do the same activity, but to try to make completely different shapes from the ones they made with the equilateral triangles.

Plenary

- Ask the children for the largest number of sides they have found. Select some children to draw their shape on the board. Talk to the children about angles and how we measure them.
- Finish the lesson by asking again what makes a triangle an equilateral triangle (all three sides are equal in length), and what makes a triangle an isosceles triangle (this triangle has two sides equal in length).

Support

- Depending on the ability of the children, it could be appropriate for them just to make the shapes and record how many sides the shape has.

Extension

- Let the children use all four triangles to make some very large shapes. Ask them to make a shape that has the biggest angle they can find rather than concentrate on the sides.

ICT Extension

- If you have a LOGO program in school and the children are quite experienced in using it, then in another lesson they could try to draw some of their shapes. This extension would give them valuable experience with the angles of their shapes.

Questions to guide assessment

- Did the children make their shapes in a systematic or random way?
- Did the children know the properties of their shapes?
- Could the children name the shapes without help?

Robots on the march

Framework for numeracy objectives

Solving problems: Reasoning about numbers and shapes

- Solve mathematical problems or puzzles, recognise and explain patterns and relationships, generalise and predict. Suggest extensions by asking 'What if...?'

Shape and space

- Begin to know that angles are measured in degrees and that one whole turn is 360° or four right angles, and a quarter turn is 90° or one right angle.

VOCABULARY

degree, right angle

Resources

- Rulers
- Photocopiable Sheets 26 to 29 (pages 67 to 70)

Oral and mental starter

Objective: Recognise which of two angles is bigger.

- Ask the children to imagine two lines, one on top of the other. One of the lines opens out slowly into an angle (demonstrate this with your hands).
- Now draw a vertical line on the board and then another line to show an angle. Give the children pencils and paper and tell them to close their eyes. Say the following:

  'Imagine that, while I count, the vertical line is going to open out to an angle. When I start counting, the angle is going to open out until I stop counting. Ready... 1, 2, 3. Open your eyes and draw the angle you saw in your head.'

- When the children have drawn the angles, ask them to compare their angle with their partners. Which one is bigger?
- Repeat this activity, counting up to different numbers.

Problem-solving challenge

How can we make a robot turn corners?

With the whole class

- This lesson will need to be taught in a large area, such as the hall. You will not need any robots! Explain to the children that the challenge is to see if they can programme a robot to carry out instructions. They will, no doubt, notice that there aren't any robots in the classroom. Tell them that they are to be the robots!
- Ask for a child volunteer to be the first robot. Go through the following instructions, with the child performing the actions:
  - Forward/backwards
  - Forward five steps
  - Backward five steps
  - Turn 360° or four right angles (remind the children what we measure angles in and what right angles are)
  - Turn 90° or a right angle
  - Turn 270° or three right angles.

  Be sure to point out that the robot can only make turns in a clockwise direction.

- Once you have taught the 'robot' these actions, give 'it' a short list of commands. The range of commands will depend on the space available, but should be something like this:

  'Forward six steps, turn 360°, forward three steps, turn 90°, forward three steps, turn 270°.'

Children working in pairs

- Using photocopiable Sheet 26 (page 67), cut up and make the cards, enough for each pair of children to have one set. Tell them they have to use all the cards to command the 'robot'. They should take turns being the robot. They have to decide the number of steps forward/backward, but limit the steps to a maximum of 10, otherwise you might 'lose' a robot. Tell the children you will be looking for the most interesting 'robot dance'!

Mini-plenary

- Ask some of the children to demonstrate how they commanded their robot. Ask the rest of the class to comment on the robot dance, whether it was correct and how it might be improved.

Children working individually

- Take the children back to the classroom and give them photocopiable Sheet 27 (page 68), which can act as a good assessment activity. The children have to record the commands to get the robot along the path.

Plenary

- Choose a target destination in the school, such as the head teacher's room, secretary's room or another classroom. Ask the children to think about the commands they would need to give the 'robot' for it to reach the target destination. Ask them to talk to their partner and write down some rough commands for getting to the target destination.
- Invite some children to read out their commands and then discuss them as a class.
- It would then be worthwhile taking the children to the target destination. Depending on staffing levels, this may need to be done in small groups.

Support

- For the 'robot dance', limit the number of cards that the children use, for example to 'Forward' and 'Turn 90°', but let them use the commands as often as they like.
- In the classroom activity, give the children Sheet 28 (page 69).

Extension

- Allow the children more sets of cards so that they can make a more complicated dance.
- For the classroom activity, give them Sheet 29 (page 70).

ICT Extension

- This is a LOGO activity and can be followed up by asking the children to construct a robot dance on the computer.

Questions to guide assessment

- Could the children use the correct commands?
- Do the children understand how we measure angles?
- Do the children understand what a right angle is?

Counting up and down

Framework for numeracy objectives

Solving problems

- Make and investigate a general statement about familiar numbers or shapes by finding examples that satisfy it.

Numbers and the number system: Properties of numbers and number sequences

- Recognise and extend number sequences formed by counting from any number in steps of constant size, extending beyond zero when counting back, for example count on in steps of 25 to 500, and then back to, say, –100.
- Recognise odd and even numbers up to 1,000, and some of their properties.

VOCABULARY

even, odd, sequence

Resources

- OHP calculator
- Class set of calculators
- Activity sheets 30 and 31 (pages 71 and 72)

Oral and mental starter

Objective: Read and write whole numbers up to 1,000.

- Set up the OHP calculator and ask the children such questions as:

  'Who can enter 789 into this calculator?'

  Then ask a child to do it.
- Say another number to the children and ask them to write it on a piece of paper. Then select a child to come out and enter that number into the calculator. Ask all the children who wrote the correct number down to hold up their piece of paper.

Problem-solving challenge

Is it possible to use addition to work out a mystery number?

With the whole class

- Teach the children how to set up a constant function on a calculator. There are two ways to do this, depending on the type of calculator. Some calculators will do it automatically. So, if you want to set up a constant function of +3, you just enter that and then press the equals key repeatedly. The calculator will then count up in threes. To enter a constant function on some calculators, you have to press the operation key twice. A small 'k' (for constant) will appear in the calculator display to show that the constant is set. Let the children explore this by entering any numbers they like.
- After the children have explored this function, set them the following challenges:
  - Enter +1 (or ++1) and press the equals key and stop at 100. Ask the children how many times they pressed the equals key.
  - Ask them to enter +2 and stop at 100. How many times did they press the equals key?
  - Ask them to enter +3 and stop at 100. Ask them why they couldn't stop at 100 and how many times they pressed the equals key.
- Show the children how to make the calculator count down by entering 100– (or – –) 1 and pressing the equals key. They will soon get into negative numbers, so ensure that they notice the negative symbol in the calculator display.
- Tell the children they are going to work in pairs to tackle the following four challenges.

Children working in pairs/individually

Count me in – Challenge 1

- One child in each pair has to enter a constant function of +? into the calculator, but not let their partner see what number they have entered. The second child is given the calculator and by pressing the equals key should be able to tell the first child what the number was. Encourage them to put in 'challenging' numbers.

Count me in – Challenge 2

- This is the same as Challenge 1, but this time counting back. For example, if Child A enters '200 – 8', Child B should be able to tell that '–8' was entered.

Count me in – Challenge 3

- Give each child a copy of photocopiable Sheet 30 (page 71). They have to complete the sheet without using a calculator. Some of them will try to calculate this mentally, others will follow the pattern.
- When they have completed the sheet, let them check it by using the constant function on the calculator. They can enter '+25' and press the equals key.

Count me in – Challenge 4

- Using the completed sheet from Challenge 3, ask the children to put a tick over every even number and a cross over every odd one. Ask them to discuss, in pairs the following statement:

  Every even number can be exactly divided by 2.

- Let the children investigate this statement using the numbers on Activity sheet 30. Let them use calculators to prove or disprove the statement.

Plenary

- Ask the children how many of them agree with the above statement about even numbers.
- As a class discuss a statement that might apply to odd numbers, such as 'If the number ends in 5 it is odd.'
- Look at the numbers in the shaded squares on Sheet 30. What can the children tell you about them?

Support

- It would be appropriate to keep the children on Challenge 1 rather than go on to Challenge 2. However, if they use photocopiable Sheet 31 (page 72), they can take part in Challenge 4.
- Point out the numbers in the shaded squares on Sheet 31. What can the children tell you about them?

Extension

- For the first part of the lesson the children could explore the constant function using multiplication and division. For Challenge 4, ask them to explore the statement for numbers over 1,000.

Questions to guide assessment

- Could the children use the calculator appropriately?
- Did all the children recognise odd and even numbers easily?
- Could the children investigate the statement about even numbers?

Odds and evens

Framework for numeracy objectives

Solving problems

- Make and investigate a general statement about familiar numbers or shapes by finding examples that satisfy it.

Numbers and the number system: Properties of numbers and number sequences

- Recognise odd and even numbers up to 1,000, and some of their properties, including the outcome of sums or differences of pairs of odd/even numbers.

Calculations

- Use known number facts and place value to add or subtract mentally, including any pair of two-digit whole numbers.
- Use informal pencil and paper methods to support, record or explain additions/subtractions.
- Develop and refine written methods for column addition and subtraction of two whole numbers less than 1,000, and addition of more than two such numbers.

VOCABULARY

difference, sum, total

Resources

- PE hoops (of two different colours)
- HTU cards
- Calculators
- Photocopiable Sheets 32 to 35 (pages 73 to 76)

Oral and mental starter

Objective: Recognise odd and even numbers.

- Put the hoops on the floor: one colour represents even numbers, the other colour represents odd numbers. Give out the HTU cards randomly and then tell the children that after you have counted to three, they have to get into a hoop of the correct colour, according to whether the number on their card is odd or even.
- When they are in the hoops, check that they are in the correct one. If some of them are in the wrong hoop, explain to them why they should be in a hoop of another colour.
- Redistribute the cards and repeat the activity.

Problem-solving challenge

Does it make a difference if a number is odd or even?

With the whole class

- Ask the children to give you five even numbers below 1,000 and five odd numbers below 1,000. Ask them how we can check that the even numbers are even and the odd numbers are odd.
- Cut out each of the statements on photocopiable Sheets 32 to 34 (pages 73 to 75) and stick them on the board or somewhere the children can see them. Explain that they are going to investigate the nine statements to see if they are correct (with the exception of statements G and I, they are all true). There are several ways to approach this activity:
  - the children work through each statement in an order you choose;
  - the children choose which statements they want to investigate;
  - the class could be divided into groups, with each group being given a statement to investigate.

However this activity is organised, explain to the children that you want them to start by investigating two-digit numbers first. Encourage them to work mentally. As they begin to explore larger numbers, they will have to use pencil and paper.

- Ask the children to complete photocopiable Sheet 35 (page 76) for each statement.

Plenary

- Go through those statements the children have worked on and discuss whether each is true or not. Either give them individual calculators or let them all use the same one.
- Ask whether the children think the statement would be true for large numbers like millions. Ask how they would know whether a number in the millions would be odd or even. Check that each statement applies to larger numbers as well.

Support

- Carefully choose the statements that you want the children to investigate. Statements that involve the sum of two numbers are the easiest. Encourage these children to record their calculations carefully, even if they calculated mentally. This will enable you to check their work more easily.

Extension

- Give the children statements that are more challenging, for example:

  'If you add three consecutive numbers the sum is always three times the middle number.'

  or:

  'The product of two consecutive numbers is always even'

Questions to guide assessment

- Did the children organise their work in a systematic way?
- Did the children use appropriate methods of calculation?
- Did the children come up with any statements of their own?

Down to zero

Framework for numeracy objectives

Solving problems

- Choose and use appropriate number operations and appropriate ways of calculating (mental, mental with jottings, pencil and paper) to solve problems.
- Solve mathematical problems or puzzles, recognise and explain patterns and relationships, generalise and predict. Suggest extensions by asking, 'What if...?'

Calculations

- Use known number facts and place value to subtract mentally, including any pair of two-digit whole numbers.
- Use informal pencil and paper methods to support, record or explain additions/subtractions.
- Develop and refine written methods for column addition and subtraction of two whole numbers smaller than 1,000.
- Check with the inverse operation.

VOCABULARY

consecutive, difference

Resources

- Activity sheet 36 (page 77)

Oral and mental starter

Objective: Add/subtract a pair of two-digit numbers.

- Write on the board a two-digit number (say, 44) and ask the children to write down an addition sum to equal the number (for example, 19 + 25) and then a similar subtraction sum (for example, 69 – 25). Ask the children for some of their answers.
- Repeat this with other two-digit numbers.

Problem-solving challenge

Is it possible to find four 'corner' numbers that can't be reduced to 0?

With the whole class

- Draw the following diagram on the board.

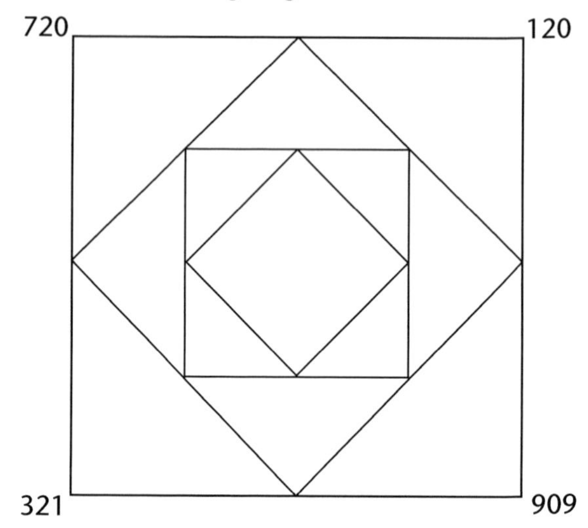

- Find the difference between the numbers in the corners to give the middle numbers.

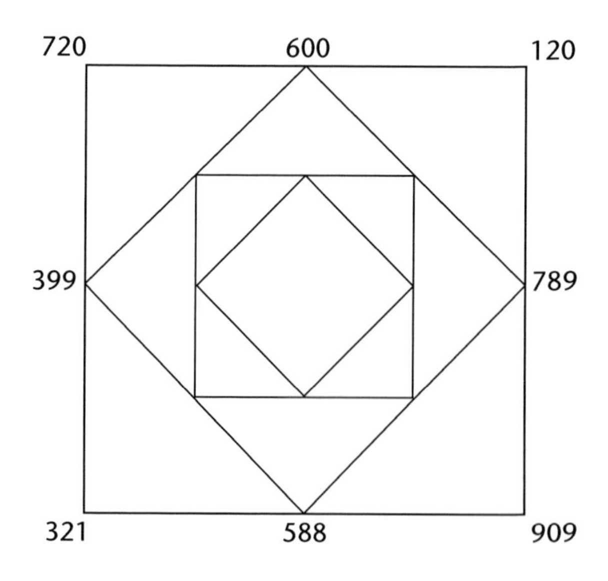

- This is repeated for the next set of numbers until you reach zero.

- Give the children copies of photocopiable Sheet 36 (page 77). Tell them the challenge is to try to find four numbers that cannot be reduced to zero. (Impossible, by the way! although some numbers will need to be reduced more times than the examples given here before they reach zero.)
- Talk to the children about the methods of subtraction they use. Some calculations they will be able to do mentally, while for others they will use informal methods (counting on, partitioning, number lines, and so on). Some children may use a formal column method if they have been taught it. Encourage the children to check their calculations by an appropriate method. In this case, using the inverse operation would be a good way.

Plenary

- Ask if any of the children found any numbers that would not diminish to zero.
- Ask the children to discuss in pairs which four three-digit numbers would give the shortest solution – any four consecutive three-digit numbers. Demonstrate this on the board.

Support

- The children can try the same challenge, but using two-digit numbers. Encourage them to try and do the calculations mentally but accept that they will be more likely to use jottings.

Extension

- Ask the children to try the same challenge but with different shapes, such as a pentagon or hexagon. Encourage them to do the calculations mentally.

Questions to guide assessment

- Which children realised that the challenge was actually impossible?
- Did the children use appropriate methods of calculation?
- Did the children use appropriate checking strategies?

Menu for Mega Bites café

The cheap but good food café

MENU

Starters

Vegetable soup	£1.50
Prawn cocktail	£2.00

Main Courses

Giant burger	£5.25
Fish fingers	£4.75
Chicken	£6.50
Chips	£1.75
Roast potatoes	£1.75
Peas	£0.80
Baked beans	£0.80

Desserts

Ice cream	£1.85
Apple pie	£2.25
Gateau	£2.80

Drinks

Cola	£0.90
Apple juice	£0.80
Orange juice	£0.80

My choices

Which foods and drinks did you choose?

How much did each item cost?

Which coins/notes did you use to pay for it?

How much change from £15 did you have left?

How did you check your answers?

Using the same coins

£1
50p
20p
10p
5p
2p
1p

Using different coins

Bigfoot – group measurements

Name	Height (in cm)	Length of foot (in cm)

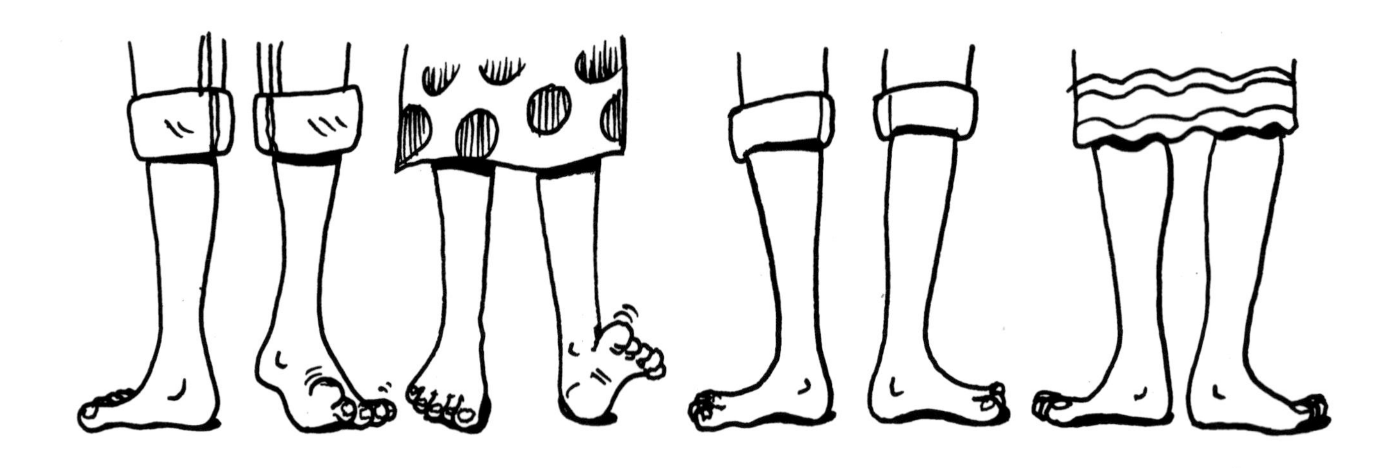

Bigfoot – class results

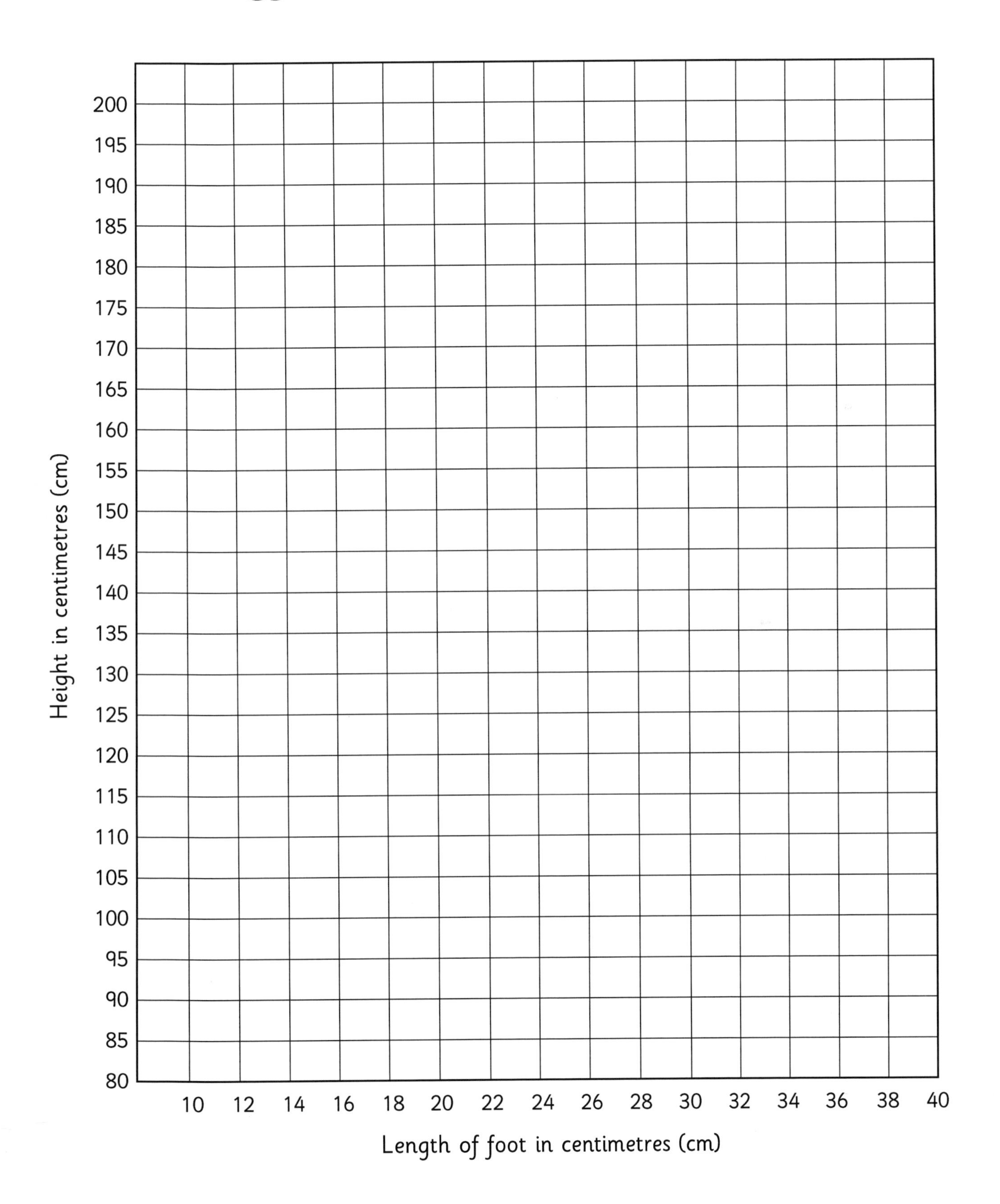

Calendar

January

1	2	3	4	5	6	7
8	9	10	11	12	13	14
15	16	17	18	19	20	21
22	23	24	25	26	27	28
29	30	31				

February

			1	2	3	4
5	6	7	8	9	10	11
12	13	14	15	16	17	18
19	20	21	22	23	24	25
26	27	28				

March

			1	2	3	4
5	6	7	8	9	10	11
12	13	14	15	16	17	18
19	20	21	22	23	24	25
26	27	28	29	30	31	

April

						1
2	3	4	5	6	7	8
9	10	11	12	13	14	15
16	17	18	19	20	21	22
23	24	25	26	27	28	29
30						

May

	1	2	3	4	5	6
7	8	9	10	11	12	13
14	15	16	17	18	19	20
21	22	23	24	25	26	27
28	29	30	31			

June

				1	2	3
4	5	6	7	8	9	10
11	12	13	14	15	16	17
18	19	20	21	22	23	24
25	26	27	28	29	30	

July

						1
2	3	4	5	6	7	8
9	10	11	12	13	14	15
16	17	18	19	20	21	22
23	24	25	26	27	28	29
30	31					

August

		1	2	3	4	5
6	7	8	9	10	11	12
13	14	15	16	17	18	19
20	21	22	23	24	25	26
27	28	29	30	31		

September

					1	2
3	4	5	6	7	8	9
10	11	12	13	14	15	16
17	18	19	20	21	22	23
24	25	26	27	28	29	30

October

1	2	3	4	5	6	7
8	9	10	11	12	13	14
15	16	17	18	19	20	21
22	23	24	25	26	27	28
29	30	31				

November

			1	2	3	4
5	6	7	8	9	10	11
12	13	14	15	16	17	18
19	20	21	22	23	24	25
26	27	28	29	30		

December

					1	2
3	4	5	6	7	8	9
10	11	12	13	14	15	16
17	18	19	20	21	22	23
24	25	26	27	28	29	30
31						

Centimetre dotted paper

Squares and triangles

Rectangles

Number walls

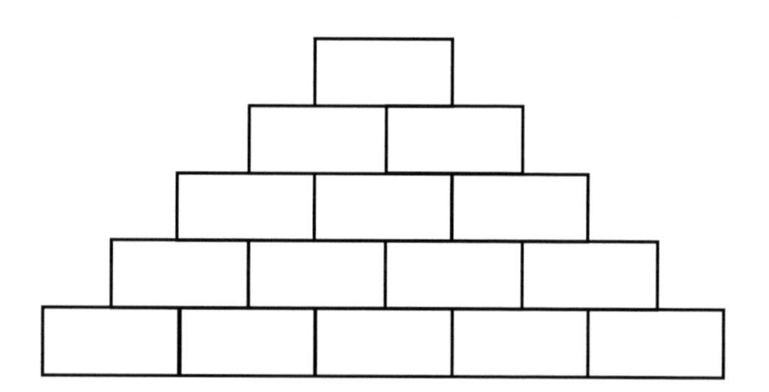

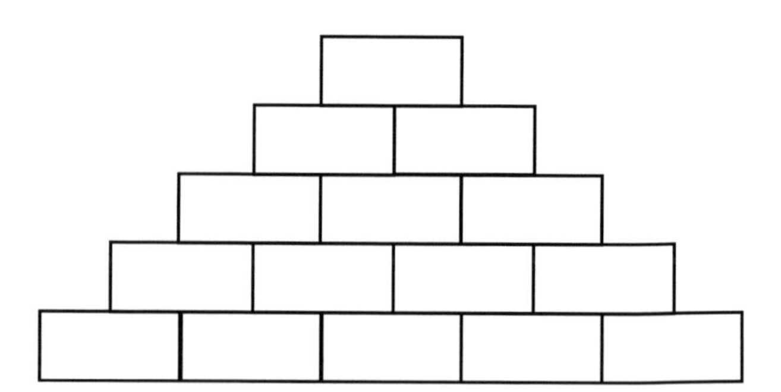

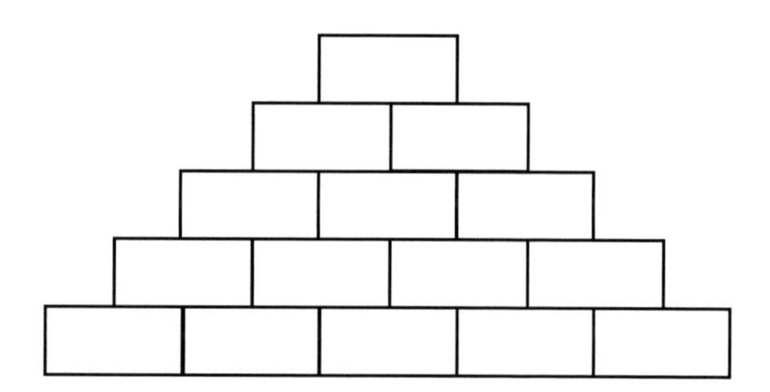

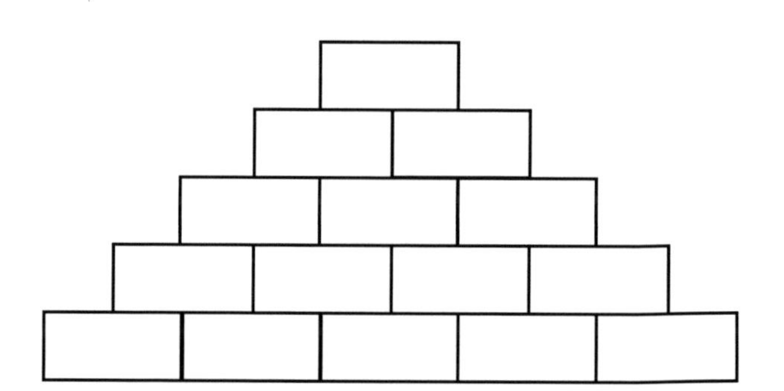

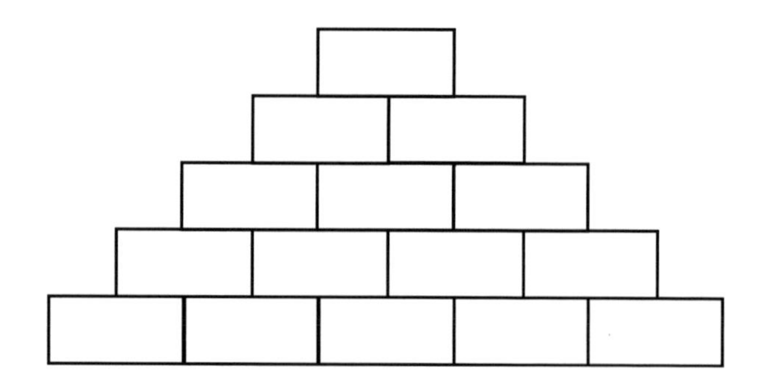

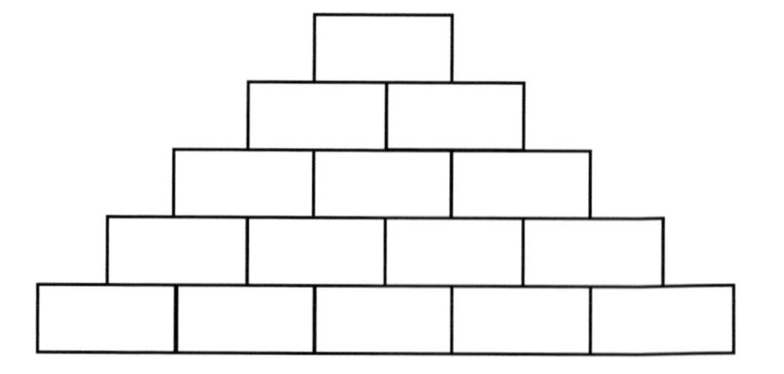

Number walls – 2

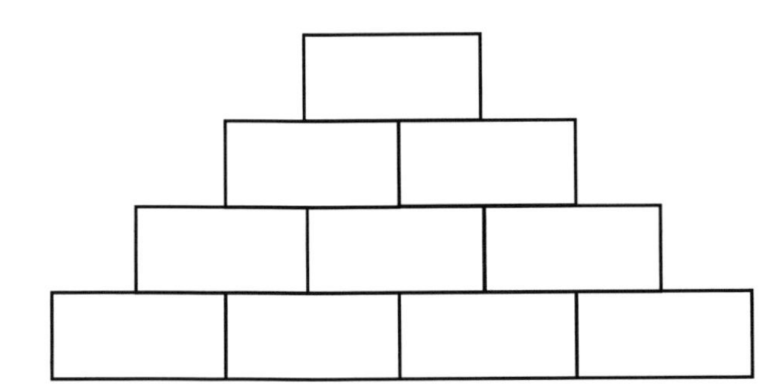

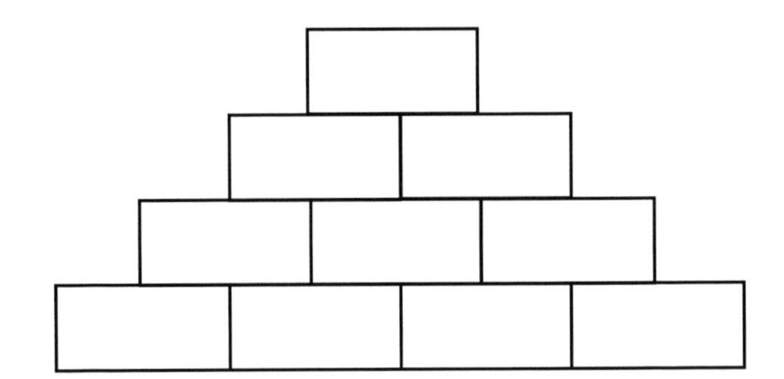

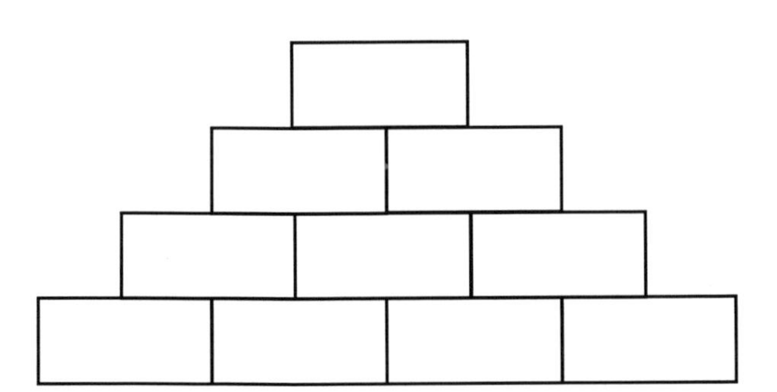

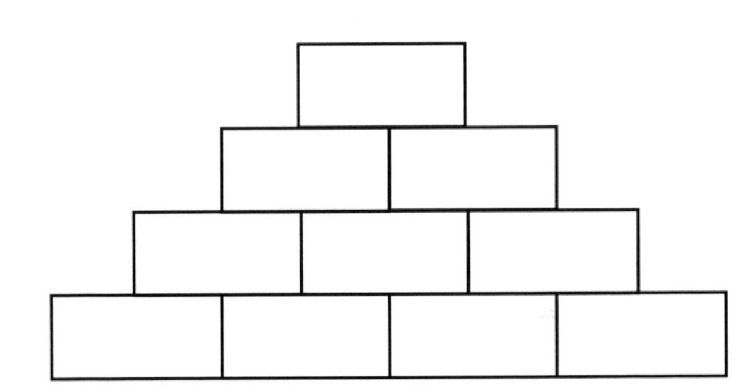

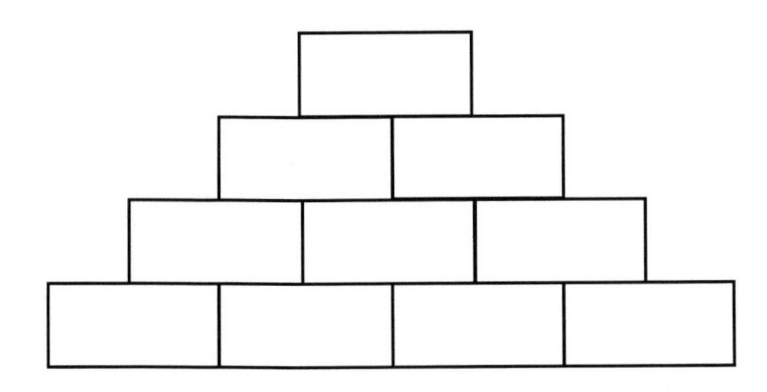

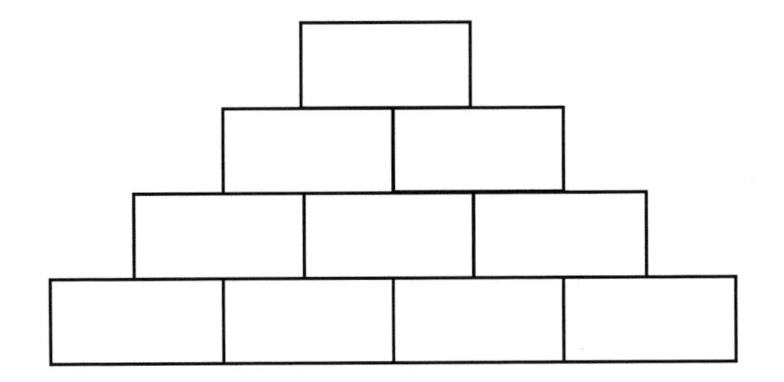

Playing the triangle

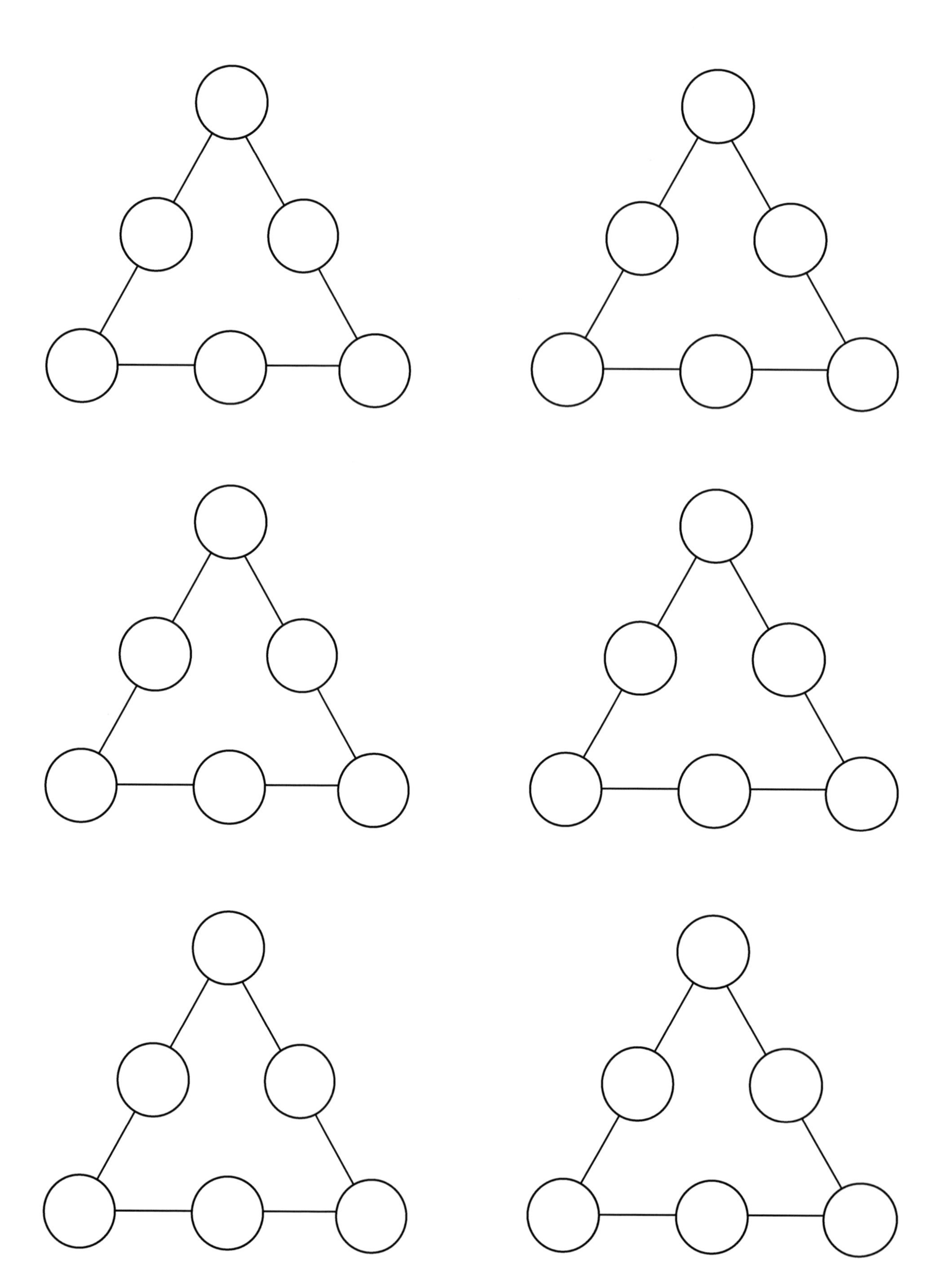

103	101	82
91	108	75
96	89	84

SHEET 15

Growing up?

Name	Age	Estimated height (m, cm)	Estimated height (cm)	Actual height (cm)	Difference (cm)	When I'm 65!

Adventure Island Activities

Activity	Price	Length of time
Abseiling	£4.75	For 1 hour
Archery	£1.80	For 15 minutes
Assault course	£1.50	For 45 minutes
Canoeing	£4.90	For 1 1/4 hours
Death slide	Free	Unlimited
Land yachting	£7.50	For 1 hour
Pony trekking	£4.20	For 1 hour
Raft building	£11.00	For 1 hour
Rock climbing	£3.75	For 1 hour
Sailing	£5.90	For 1 hour

Adventure Island Activities

Activity	Price	Length of time
Abseiling	£5.00	For 1 hour
Archery	£2.00	For 15 minutes
Assault course	£2.00	For 45 minutes
Canoeing	£5.00	For 1 1/4 hours
Death slide	Free	Unlimited
Land yachting	£7.00	For 1 hour
Pony trekking	£4.00	For 1 hour
Raft building	£10.00	For 1 hour
Rock climbing	£3.00	For 1 hour
Sailing	£6.00	For 1 hour

Adventure Island Activities

Activity	Price	Length of time
Abseiling	£4.01	For 1 hour
Archery	£1.88	For 15 minutes
Assault course	£1.55	For 45 minutes
Canoeing	£4.99	For 1 1/4 hours
Death slide	Free	Unlimited
Land yachting	£7.30	For 1 hour
Pony trekking	£4.25	For 1 hour
Raft building	£11.11	For 1 hour
Rock climbing	£3.75	For 1 hour
Sailing	£5.99	For 1 hour

Adventure Island Activities

Name ______________________________

Day of the week	Session 1	Session 2	Session 3	Session 4
Monday				
Tuesday				
Wednesday				
Cost				

Total cost of the activities =

Change from £50.00 =

Number clouds

Use +21, –19, x5 or ÷3 to link each number in cloud A to a number in cloud B. Draw a line between the numbers. One has been done for you.

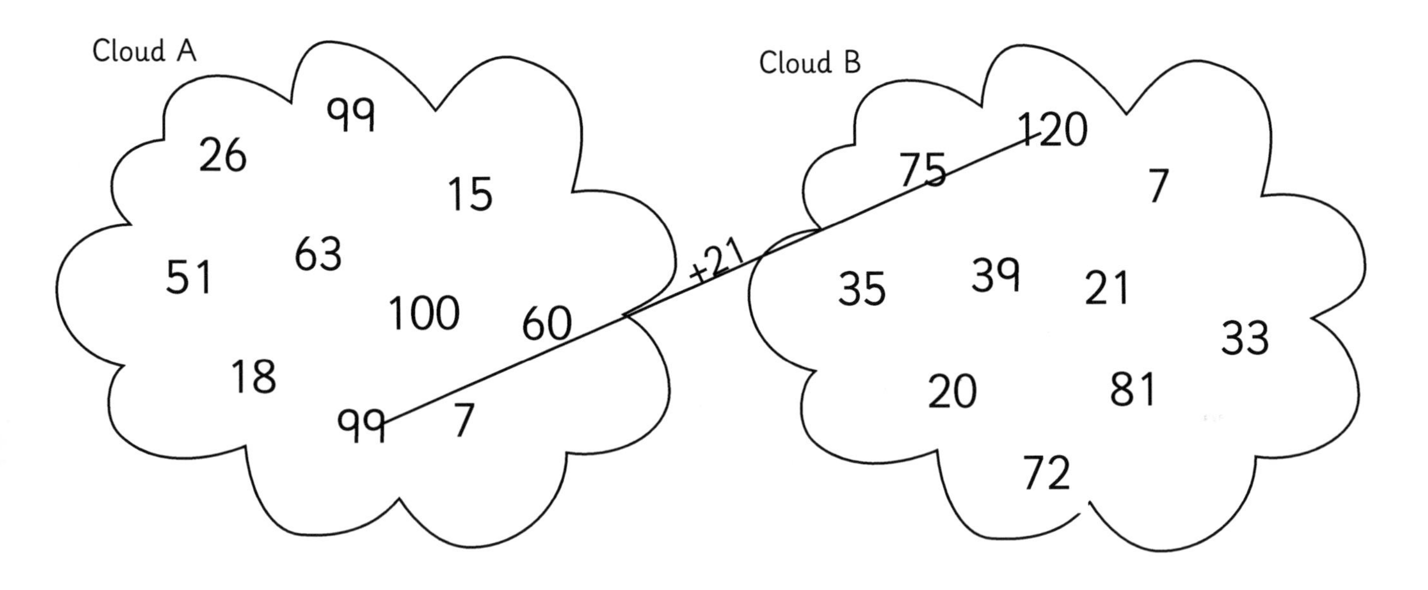

Now use +16, –9, x3 or ÷4 to link each number in cloud C to a number in cloud D. Draw a line between the numbers.

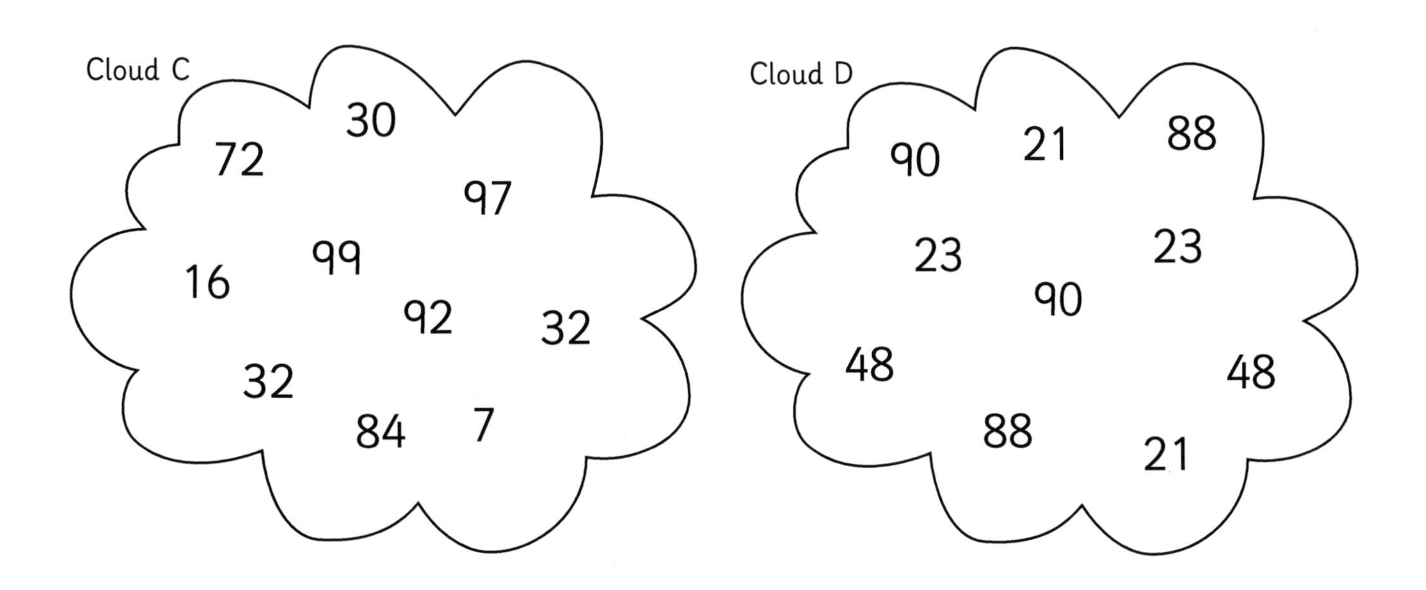

Number clouds

	+/x			−/÷		
26			52			2
88			121			22
20			100			0
13			39			29
60			240			60
17			75			15
98			196			97
52			100			25

Equilateral triangles

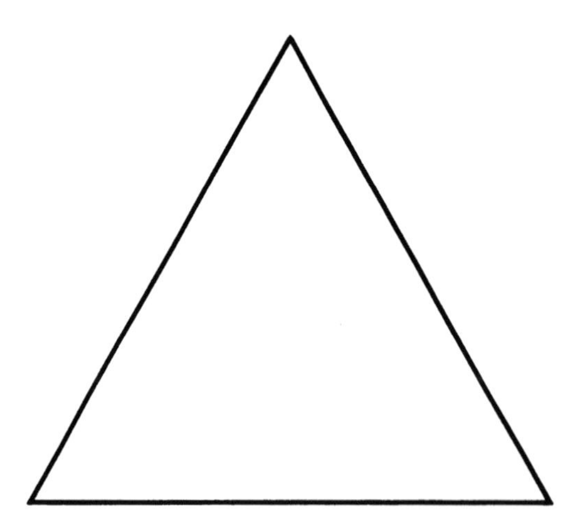

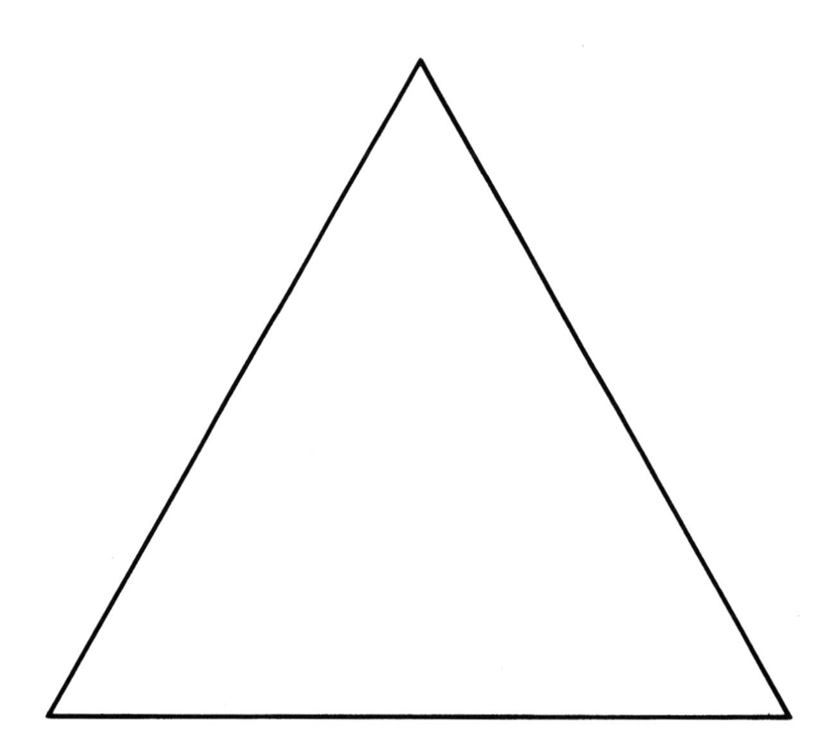

Isosceles triangles

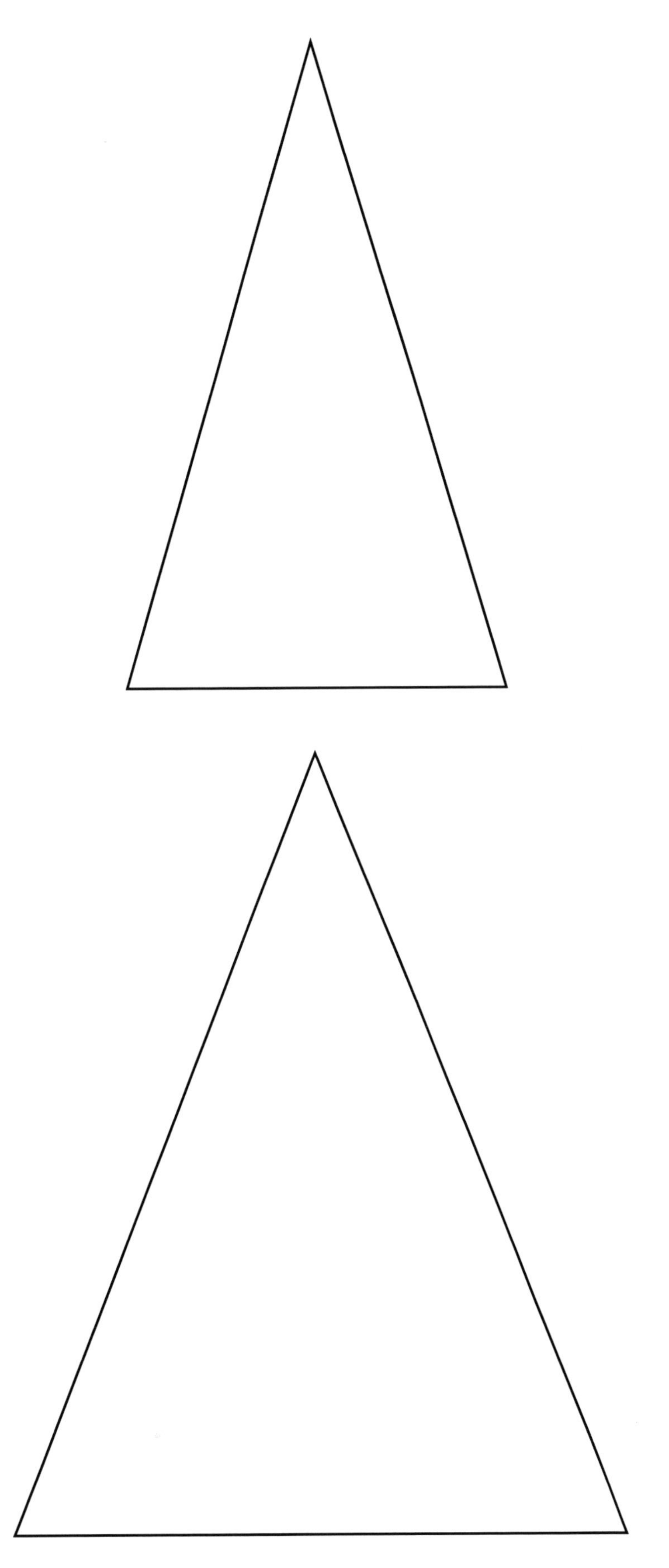

Sketch of shape	Sketch of shape	Sketch of shape	Sketch of shape
Name of shape ____________	Name of shape ____________	Name of shape ____________	Name of shape ____________
Number of sides ________	Number of sides ________	Number of sides ________	Number of sides ________
Number of angles ________	Number of angles ________	Number of angles ________	Number of angles ________
Symmetry ✔/✘ ________	Symmetry ✔/✘ ________	Symmetry ✔/✘ ________	Symmetry ✔/✘ ________
Regular ✔/✘ ________	Regular ✔/✘ ________	Regular ✔/✘ ________	Regular ✔/✘ ________

Forward	Backward
Turn 360°	Turn 90°
Turn 270°	Forward

Robot path – 1

Name ______________________________

Guide the robot along the path. Use these commands:
Forward (1 = 1 cm), turn 90°, turn 270°, and so on.
Write your commands in this box.

Robot path – 2

Name ____

Guide the robot along the path. Use these commands:
Forward (1 = 1 cm), turn 90°, turn 270°, and so on.
Write your commands in this box.

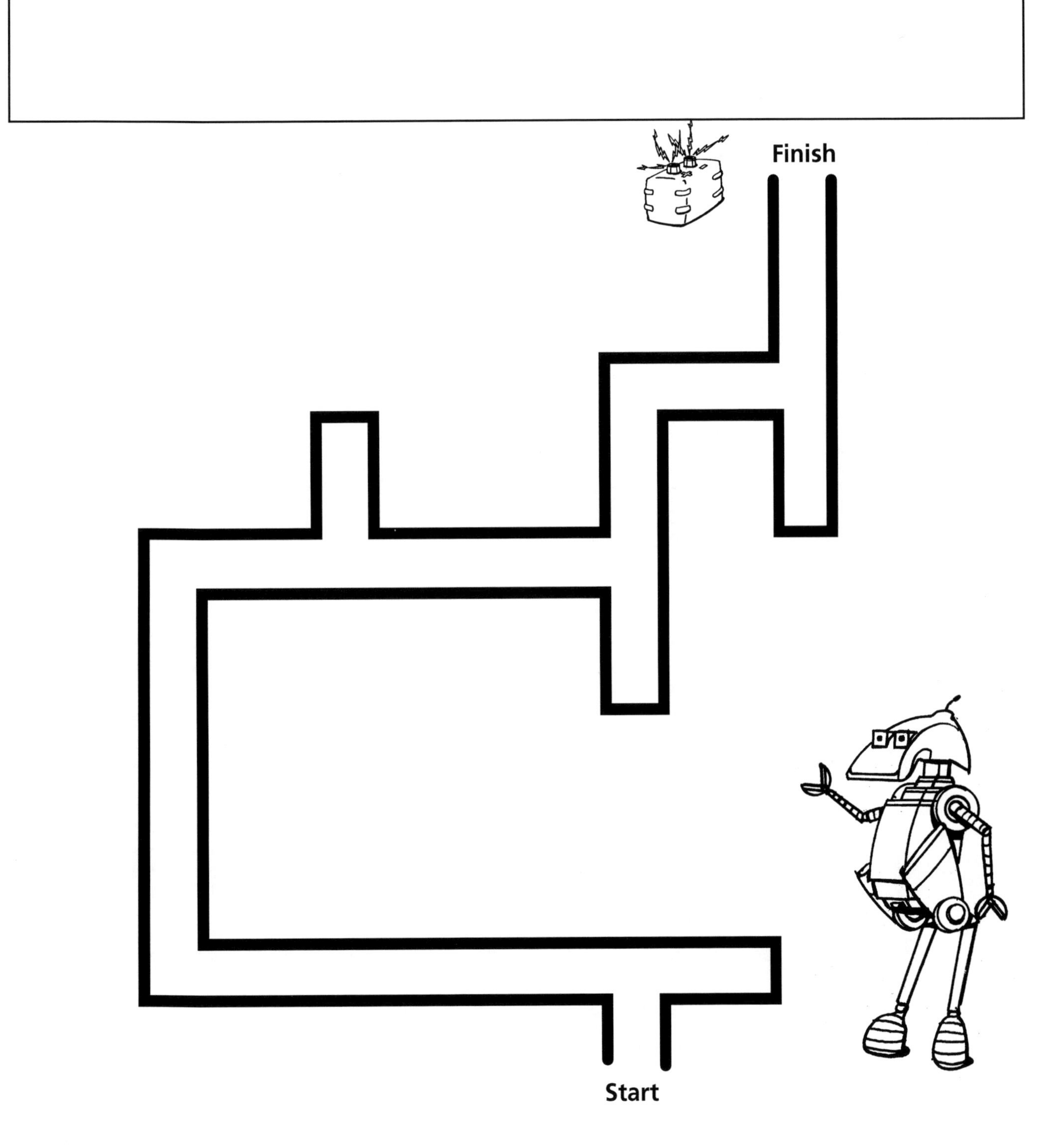

Robot path – 3

Name ______________________________

Guide the robot along the path. Use these commands:
Forward (1 = 1 cm), turn 90°, turn 270°, and so on.
Write your commands in this box.

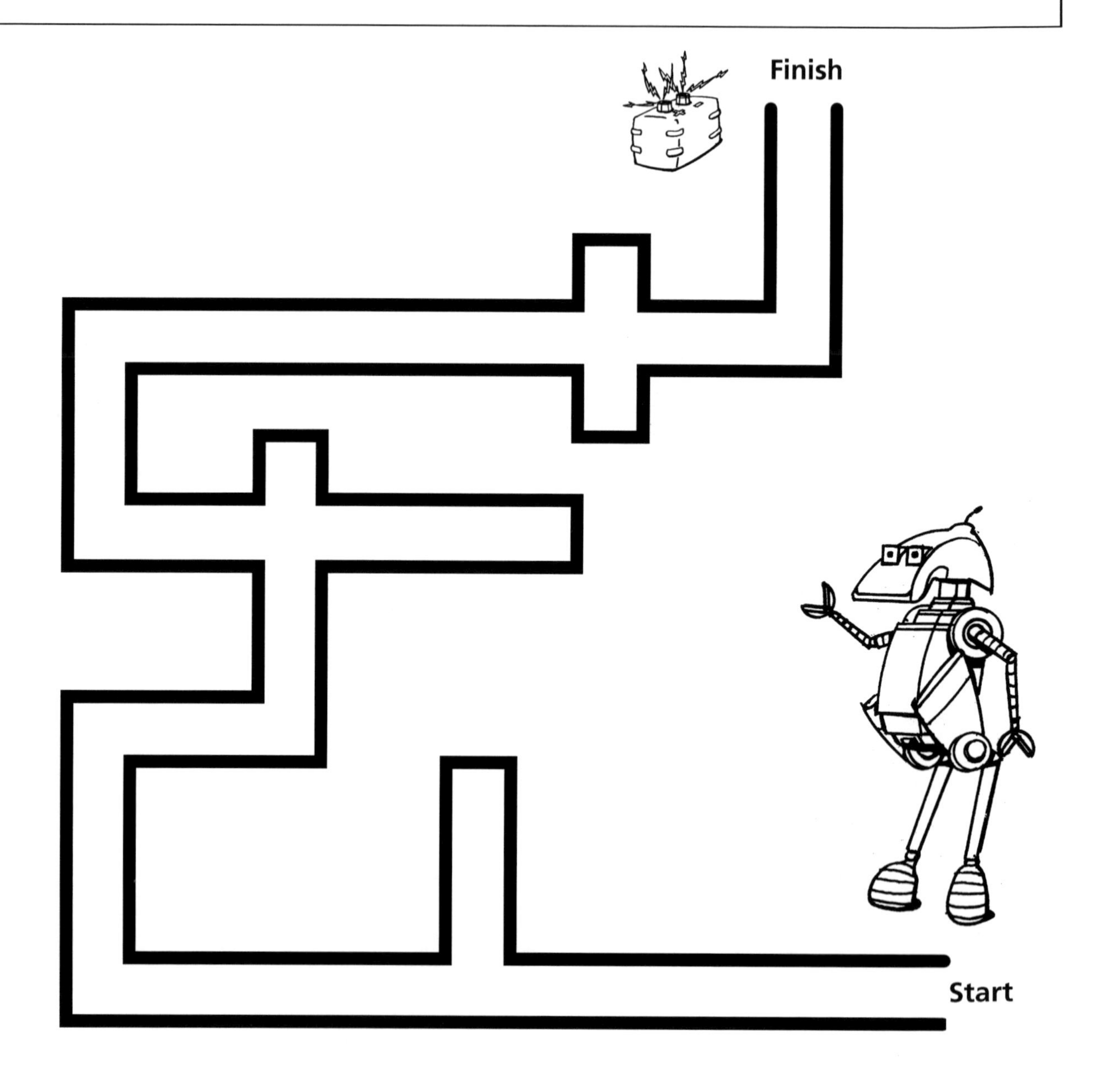

Name ______________________________

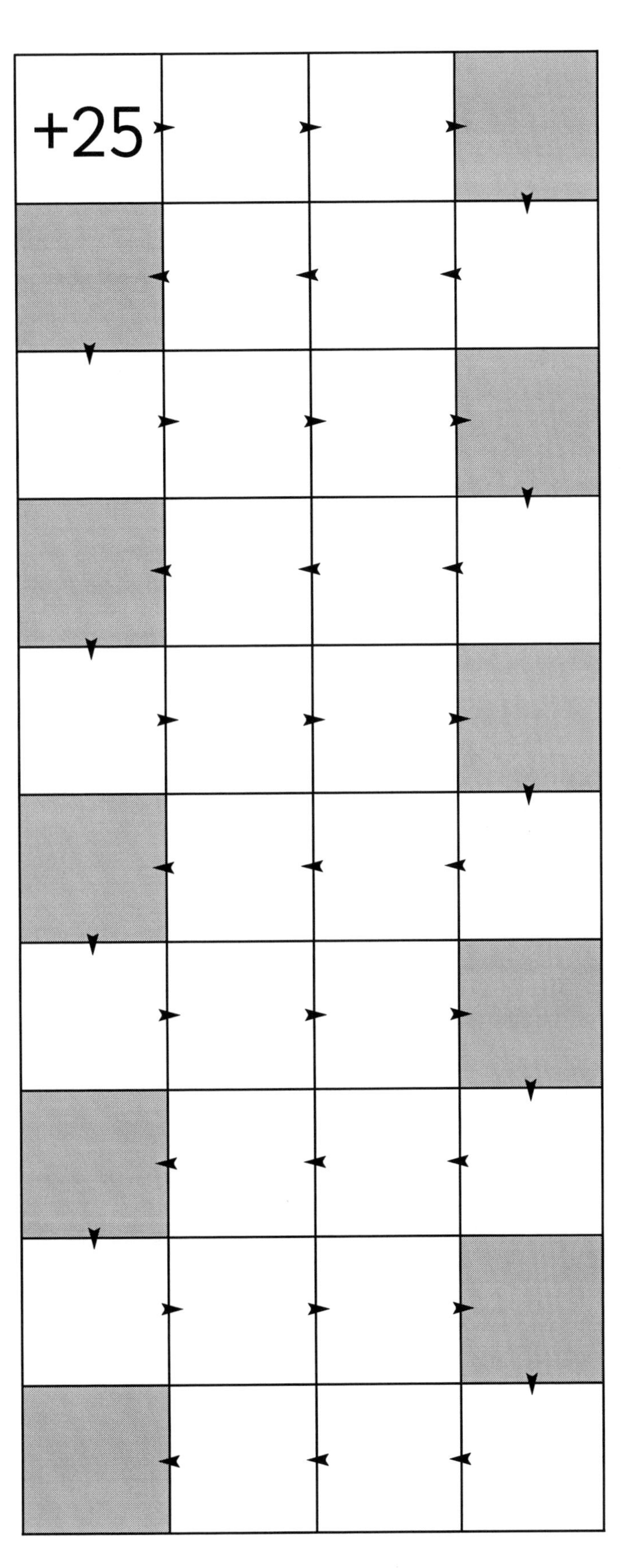

Name ______________________________

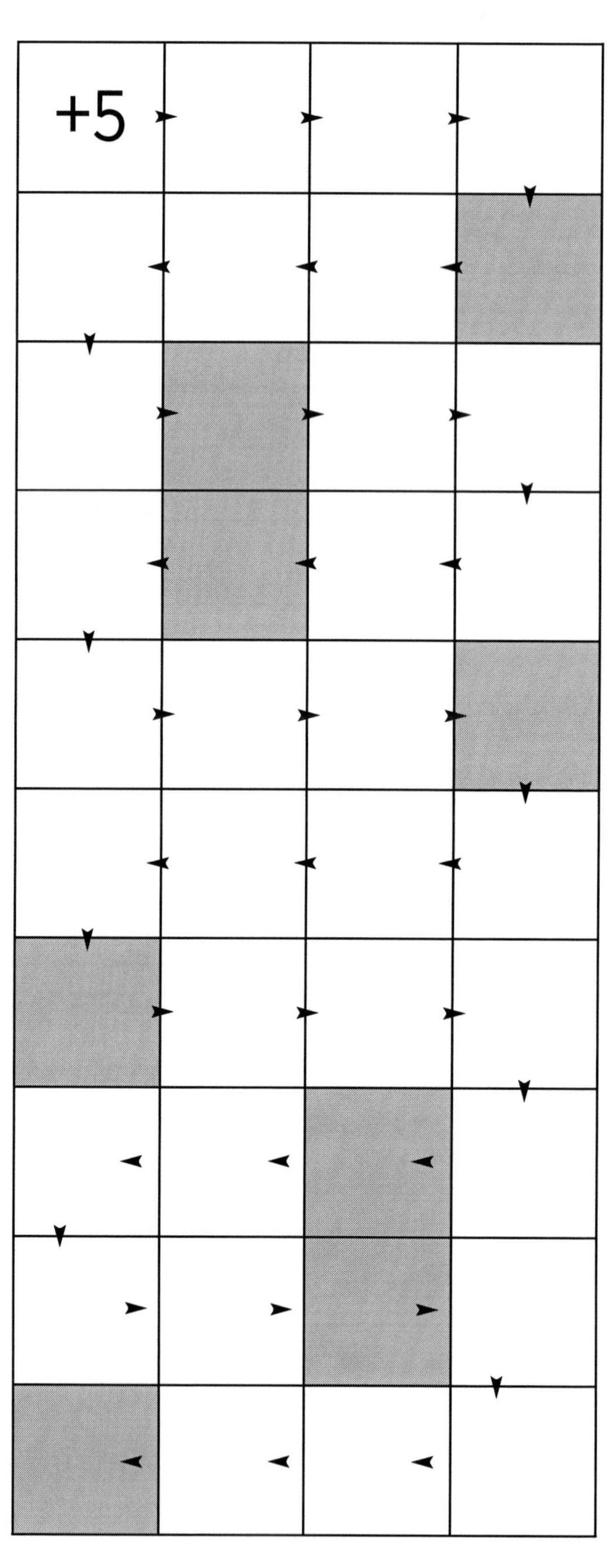

A

If you double any odd number the answer is always an even number.

B

If you double any even number the answer is always an even number.

C

The sum of an odd and even number is always an odd number.

D

The difference between an even number and an odd number is always an odd number.

E

The difference between two odd numbers is always an even number.

F

The difference between two even numbers is always an even number.

G

The sum of three odd numbers is always an even number.

H

The sum of two odd numbers and one even number is always an even number.

I

The sum of two even numbers and one odd number is always an even number.

SHEET 35

Name ______________________________

Today I investigated this statement:

Here are some of my calculations:

I think that the statement is true because:

I think that the statement is not true because:

Name ______________________________

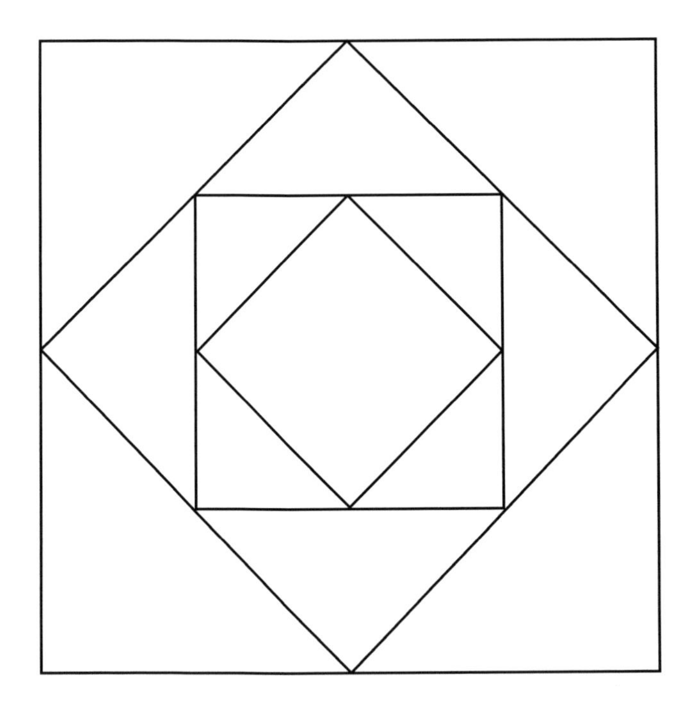

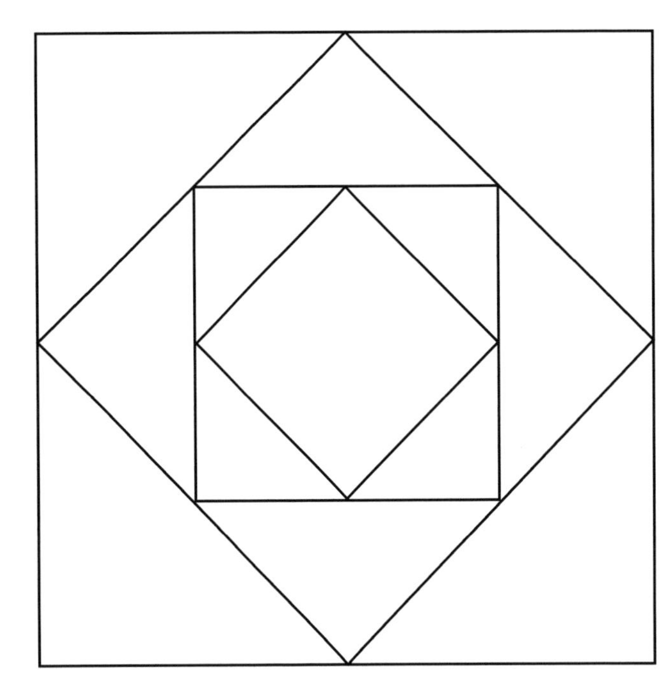

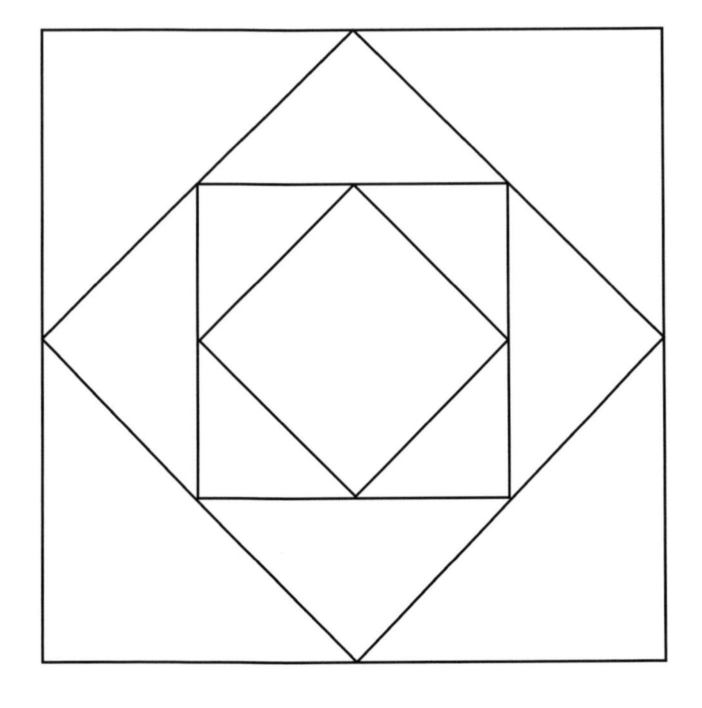

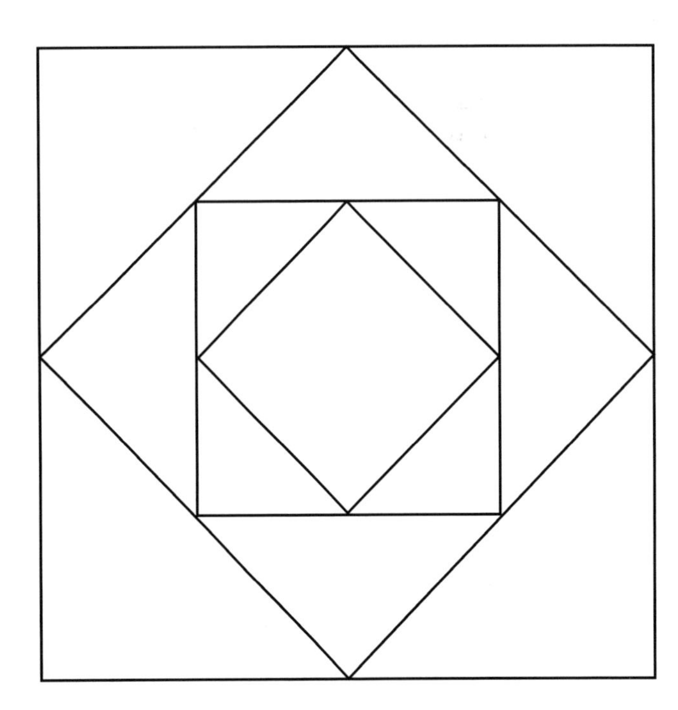

100 square

1	2	3	4	5	6	7	8	9	10
11	12	13	14	15	16	17	18	19	20
21	22	23	24	25	26	27	28	29	30
31	32	33	34	35	36	37	38	39	40
41	42	43	44	45	46	47	48	49	50
51	52	53	54	55	56	57	58	59	60
61	62	63	64	65	66	67	68	69	70
71	72	73	74	75	76	77	78	79	80
81	82	83	84	85	86	87	88	89	90
91	92	93	94	95	96	97	98	99	100

Number track

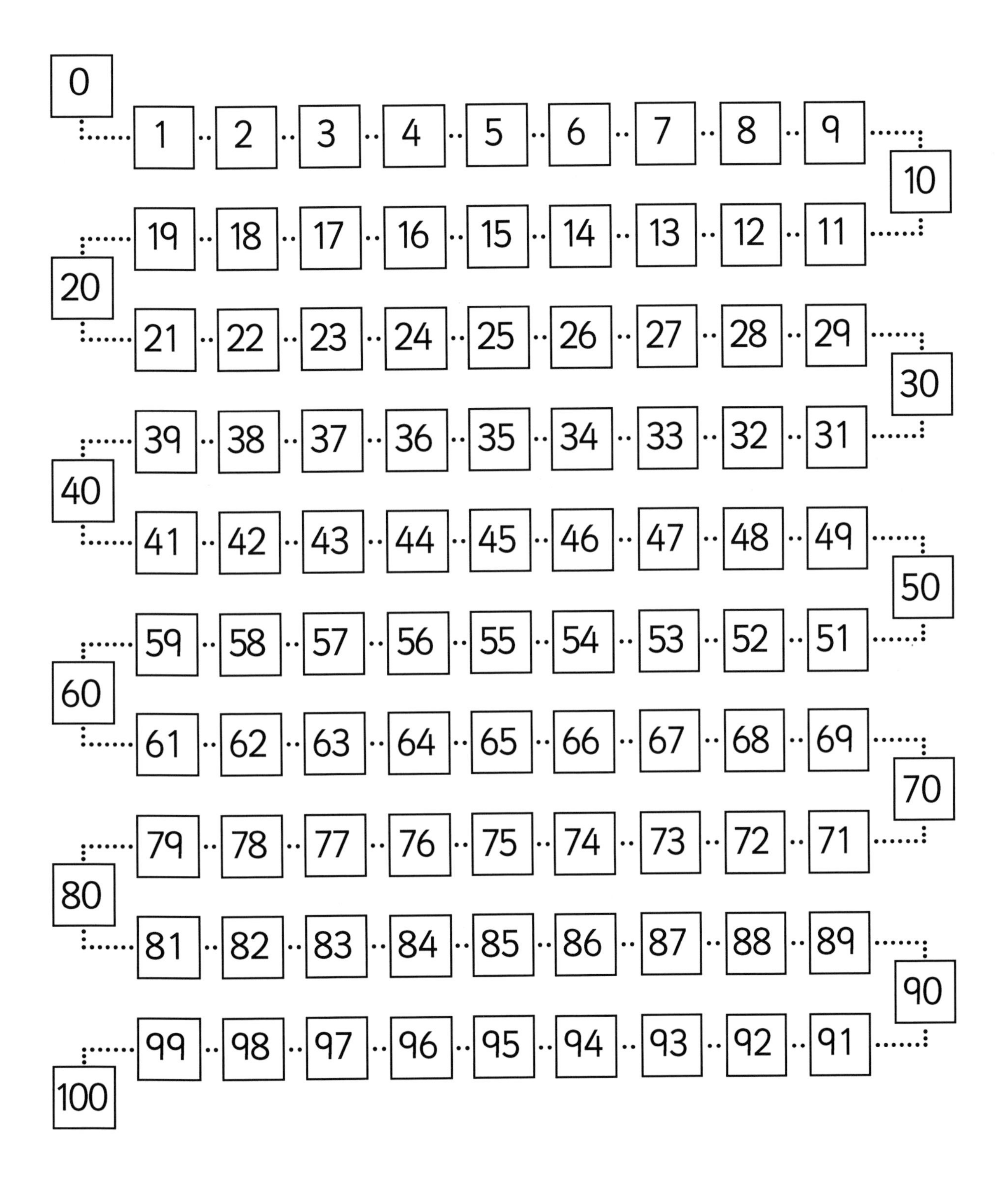

Tables square

X	0	1	2	3	4	5	6	7	8	9	10
0											
1											
2											
3											
4											
5											
6											
7											
8											
9											
10											